A NEW DIRECTION

A Cognitive-Behavioral Treatment Curriculum

LONG-TERM
FACILITATOR'S GUIDE

Criminal & Addictive Thinking

Mapping a Life
of Recovery & Freedom
for Chemically Dependent
Criminal Offenders

**A Collaboration of Chemical Dependency Professionals from
the Minnesota Department of Corrections and the Hazelden Foundation**

HAZELDEN

Hazelden
Center City, Minnesota 55012-0176

1-800-328-9000
1-651-213-4590 (Fax)
www.hazelden.org

©2002 by Hazelden Foundation
All rights reserved. Published 2002
Printed in the United States of America

Cover design by David Spohn
Interior design by Terri Kinne
Illustrations by Patrice Barton

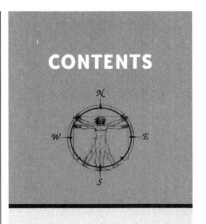

CONTENTS

A NEW DIRECTION

A Cognitive-Behavioral Treatment Curriculum

Acknowledgments

The following people, whose titles and positions are listed as held upon publication, have contributed to this curriculum:

Sheryl Ramstad Hvass
Commissioner, Minnesota Department of Corrections

Peter Bell
Executive Vice President, Hazelden Publishing and Educational Services

James D. Kaul, Ph.D.
Director, TRIAD Chemical Dependency Program
Minnesota Department of Corrections

Will Alexander
Sex Offender/Chemical Dependency Services Unit, Minnesota Department of Corrections

We are also indebted to Stanton Samenow, Ph.D., for his pioneering work on criminal thinking.

Minnesota Department of Corrections

Sex Offender Treatment Program at Lino Lakes Minnesota Correctional Facility
Robin Goldman, Director
Jim Berg, Program Supervisor
Brian Heinsohn, Corrections Program Therapist
Greg Kraft, Corrections Program Therapist
K. Kaprice Borowski Krebsbach, Corrections Program Therapist
Kevin Nelson, Corrections Program Therapist
Tim Schrupp, Corrections Program Therapist
Pamela Stanchfield, Corrections Program Therapist
Jason Terwey, Corrections Program Therapist
John Vieno, Corrections Program Therapist
Cynthia Woodward, Corrections Program Therapist

TRIAD Chemical Dependency Program at Lino Lakes Minnesota Correctional Facility
Launie Zaffke, Supervisor
Randy Tenge, Supervisor
Carmen Ihlenfeldt, Acting Supervisor
Thomas A. Berner, Corrections Program Therapist
Toni Brezina, Corrections Program Therapist
Jeanie Cook, Corrections Program Therapist
Ronald J. DeGidio, Corrections Program Therapist
Susan DeGidio, Corrections Program Therapist
Maryann Edgerley, Corrections Program Therapist
Connie Garritsen, Corrections Program Therapist
Gerald Gibcke, Corrections Program Therapist
Anthony Hoheisel, Corrections Program Therapist
Deidra Jones, Corrections Program Therapist

Beth Matchey, Corrections Program Therapist
Jack McGee, Corrections Program Therapist
Laurie Merth, Corrections Program Therapist
Jackie Michaelson, Corrections Program Therapist
Hal Palmer, Corrections Program Therapist
Terrance Peach, Corrections Program Therapist
Holly Petersen, Corrections Program Therapist
Linda Rose, Corrections Program Therapist
Kathy Thompson, Corrections Program Therapist
Beverly Welo, Corrections Program Therapist

Reshape Chemical Dependency Program at Saint Cloud Minnesota Correctional Facility

Robert L. Jungbauer, Director
Christine Fortson, Corrections Program Therapist
Tracanne Nelson, Corrections Program Therapist
Jeffrey D. Spies, Corrections Program Therapist

Atlantis Chemical Dependency Program at Stillwater Minnesota Correctional Facility

Bob Reed, Director
Dennis Abitz, Corrections Program Therapist
Bill Burgin, Corrections Program Therapist
Tom Shipp, Corrections Program Therapist

New Dimensions Chemical Dependency Program at Faribault Minnesota Correctional Facility

Michael Coleman, Supervisor
Michele Caron, Corrections Program Therapist
Judy Squire, Corrections Program Therapist
Shirley Behrends, Corrections Program Therapist

Central Office

Jim Linehan, Corrections Program Therapist

Minnesota Department of Corrections Supervising Agents

Russ Stricker, Correctional Unit Supervisor
Bobbi Chevaliar-Jones, Intensive Supervised Release Agent
William Hafner, Corrections Agent
Gregory Fletcher, 180 Degrees Halfway House

In Addition:

Writers: Corrine Casanova, Deborah Johnson, Stephen Lehman, Joseph M. Moriarity, Paul Schersten.
Designer: Terri Kinne. **Typesetters:** Terri Kinne, Julie Szamocki. **Illustrator:** Patrice Barton.
Prepress: Don Freeman, Kathryn Kjorlien, Rachelle Kuehl, Joan Seim, Tracy Snyder, David Spohn.
Editor: Corrine Casanova. **Copy editors:** Monica Dwyer Abress, Kristal Leebrick, Caryn Pernu.
Proofreaders: Catherine Broberg, Kristal Leebrick. **Training Consultant:** Derick Crim **Video production manager:** Alexis Scott.

Special thanks: Any Color Painting Company; Blue Moon Production Company; Eden Re-entry Services; inmates and staff of Lino Lakes, Rush City, and Stillwater Minnesota Correctional Facilities.

Facilitator Introduction

Each program must determine what level of therapeutic support to provide its inmate participants. The depth of the therapeutic relationship should determine the level of introspection encouraged by programming staff.

For example, a therapeutic community that offers a low ratio of inmates to therapist, provides for group therapy several times weekly, and is supported by psychological services is a "safe" environment for inmate participants to explore issues relating to sexual abuse in childhood. Large psycho-educational programs with limited therapist-client interactions and few psychological services should take great care in addressing issues that may cause the inmate to become overwhelmed and unsafe in the general population. For this reason, cognitive-behavioral therapies are particularly useful with inmate populations. The traditional chemical dependency model (which stresses the need for feelings, identification, and congruence) may actually put the inmate population at risk.

This workbook is written at a sixth-grade reading level. Portions are reading-intense. We have tried to limit this as much as possible. We suggest that you read these sections, if possible, as a group using some of your better readers. If you have access to tutors, have them assist the participants who have trouble reading and understanding the points being made. Another option is to have the participants work in teams of two. They can read each page out loud together and then discuss it. Each member of the team then initials the pages in the two workbooks for purposes of accountability. This will help those with lower reading levels to process the ideas being presented.

All three of the *A New Direction* videos included with this module were created as therapeutic tools. The *Criminal & Addictive Behavior: Tactics* video shows the link between addictive and criminal thinking and common criminal tactics used. The *Thinking About Your Thinking, Part I* video examines individual components of the Thinking Report during and actual group session. In the *Thinking About Your Thinking, Part 2* video, eight scenarios/role plays help teach participants how to effectively work through Thinking Reports. Finally, because of space limitations in this workbook, participants will not always have enough space to write all that they need to when doing the exercises. We suggest that they use a notebook (rather than loose sheets of paper) to do additional exercises when necessary. We have numbered the exercises consecutively. Using a bound notebook will help them keep track of their work and will be easier for you to evaluate, too.

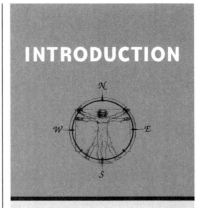

Mapmaking

*Your **best** thinking is what got you here.*

Thinking is how we get around and function in the world. It's what directs us to do one thing rather than another, to go here and not there, to say this and not that. Thinking is how we **interact** with the world.

Facilitator Note
It is important that the participants cover the ideas in this section, either in lecture or as a reading assignment, **before** they try to do the exercises.

First, the world provides us with *experiences* that we take in with our senses—sight, hearing, touch, taste, smell, and intuition. Next, we *process* that information—we make sense of it for ourselves—through our thinking. And finally, our thinking shows how we will *respond* to the world—what we will do or say, or not do or say.

This thought process—taking in information, thinking about what it means and how to respond, and then acting upon that thinking—is what sets human beings apart from other animals. While other animals have some kind of thought processes related to survival, reproduction, and avoiding pain, only humans have the ability to think about their thoughts.

Interact means that two or more things act back and forth on each other. Participants in a therapeutic community group *interact*—they take in information from each other, are changed by it, and give feedback. A healthy person *interacts* with the world.

As a criminal and an addict, however, you haven't been thinking about your own thoughts very much or very well. In fact, you have been impulsive, selfish, abusive, disconnected from people, and arrogant. You've been behaving like less than the human being you could be. As a result, you are suffering negative consequences.

As one inmate put it to another,

> *"Man, you just don't get it.*
> *You're **incarcerated.***
> *You been kicked out of the **world.**"*

Look around you. You are lost, and you don't know why. You need to find out why you've been "kicked out of the world." You need a good map to find your way out of this maze. You need to become fully human again.

Thought Maps

It's still possible for you to change your thinking. Thinking is the tool people use to create a mental map of the outside world: what it is like, where the boundaries are, and where it is safe or dangerous.

We develop our own personal mental map as we are growing up. To do so, we use the information we take in starting from the day we are born. This information is made up of everything that goes on around us and our responses to it. Our personal mental map consists of all the things we encounter in life—interactions with parents, teachers, neighbors, strangers, authorities, friends, relatives, people we never meet but only hear about, nature, television, stories we read or hear, movies, music, art, history, and other parts of our culture.

Often, we don't even realize when we are adding to our map by learning something new or reinforcing a previous experience. Mental mapmaking happens unconsciously and goes on *constantly.* It is going on right now.

■

Facilitator Note

Our mental maps include our beliefs, attitudes, and assumptions about ourselves, others, and the world. They guide our behavior and give us direction.

Using a Map

What are maps for? Imagine a road map, either one someone drew for you or one you would get at a gas station or find in an atlas. Think about what road maps are for and how we use them.

➤ Describe how you would use such a map and why you would need it.

_____

_____

_____

_____

_____

_____

_____

Now imagine that the map you are using is not completely right. It is outdated; things have changed since it was drawn. New roads were built and old ones closed down. Also, the people who drew this map didn't have all the information they needed, or some of the information they had was wrong, or they were sloppy in their work. Because of all this, a few roads and landmarks are labeled incorrectly.

➤ What are some of the possible consequences of following
an inaccurate map?

1. _____

_____

2. _____

_____

3. _____

_____

Not all maps are the same.

Figure 1

Figure 2

Figure 3

Despite their differences, each of these maps represents the same area of land, which we recognize as the United States. Each map attempts to tell the truth about that land area. Obviously, however, each is very different in the type and quality of information it provides.

➤ What are some differences between the three maps?

1. _____

   _____

   _____

2. _____

   _____

   _____

3. _____

   _____

   _____

4. _____

   _____

   _____

Facilitator Note

Participants may get stuck on the visual distinctions between the maps. This exercise, however, aims to get them to look at the practical distinctions between them: how the maps are used differently, how each has a distinct purpose. When people use the wrong mental map in the wrong situation, they get poor results.

Example: The mental map they use to survive in the correctional institution will not serve them on the outside.

Each map represents the land area called the United States, yet each has a different value and purpose. Keep in mind that these maps are not the United States itself; they are *representations* of it. Not only that, as you can see, each map has its limitations and distortions.

These maps are not reality.
Each one is merely a different
***representation* of reality.**

The same is true of your own personal mental map. And just as each of these three maps has flaws and limitations, so does your personal mental map. Even though your inner map has distortions and areas that are incomplete, *it's all you've got.* It gives you direction, shows you where you are located in respect to the rest of the world, and ultimately guides your behavior. It tells you which way to go and shows the different paths you can take to get there. It also indicates what to look out for (landmarks and obstacles) along the way.

Trying to Navigate with Faulty Maps

You also use thinking to figure out the strengths and weaknesses of your body, your mind, and your ***spirit of life.*** Think of your body, mind, and spirit of life as a car you ride around the world in. You might be a Mercedes, you might be a Ford, or you might be an old wreck. (You might be an old wreck and *think* you are a Mercedes!) To some extent, you get the "car" you were born with. However, the thinking choices you make will determine how well the car runs. If you take care of your body, mind, and spirit of life, your "car" will work better and run longer. If you don't take care of it, it will break down and give you a lot of trouble.

Thinking, then, is (1) how you map the world and (2) how you get around in it. But here's the catch: *what you think is not always right.*

People are capable of wonderfully creative and useful thoughts. They are also capable of making terrible errors in their thinking, errors that can cause pain, humiliation, guilt and remorse, and loss of freedom. Sometimes your mental map of the world is simply wrong, and when you follow it—thinking it will take you to pleasure and safety and abundance—you find yourself in quicksand or over a cliff.

**With a faulty map,
the pathway to paradise can
turn out to be the road to ruin.**

■

Spirit of Life

Your *spirit of life* is the spark in you that keeps your heart pumping, brain working, muscles moving, and blood circulating. It is the difference between a live body and a dead one. Some people call it soul, spirit, ghost, or just life principle. What you call it and how you think about it is up to you. The most important thing to know about your spirit of life is that you have one—that it's a part of who you are.

With an inaccurate map, you can get lost in the world, have one bad experience after another, and get more and more hurt, frustrated, and miserable.

■

All this is the bad news, and it explains why you are reading this while incarcerated. Your thought map didn't work for you—it led you to where you are right now.

Constructing a New Thought Map

The good news is, you're in charge of your mental map. You can figure out which parts of your old, faulty mental map don't work. Then you can learn how to begin the process of erasing those parts and start creating new, effective maps. Will it take effort? Yes. Can you do it? Yes, you can—*if you make that decision.*

Many, many people in situations similar to yours have done it. This workbook will give you the tools you'll need and teach you how to use them—if you do the work. The therapists and instructors of this program will provide guidance and direction—if you accept what they have to offer. It's your choice.

Drugs, dishonesty, denial—those are the thought maps that got you where you are today: behind bars. Addicted to alcohol or other drugs. Separated from family, distrustful even of your so-called friends. Angry at the world, angry at society, angry at judges and prosecutors, angry at family, angry at staff, angry at fellow inmates. Angry at yourself (maybe). Your old thought map has led you into the woods, and sooner or later, if you continue to follow it, it will lead you over a cliff.

This treatment program offers you help in writing a better map. It will teach you how to begin to change *what* you think and *how* you think. Three ideas sum up the workbook's basic approach:

1. Our thinking greatly influences our feelings and our behavior.

2. We can learn to monitor our thinking (to think about our thinking) and change it.

3. Our behavior patterns will change based upon the changes in our thinking patterns.

■

Keep the following in mind as you move through this workbook. It's an important concept.

There are problems, and there are the ways you choose to handle these problems. They are two different things. What often gets you into trouble isn't always the problems you face but how you respond to them.

Creating new thought maps *will* take effort, but over time you'll see the benefits. Nobody likes change, but change is just a part of being human, and no one can escape it, not even the richest and most powerful or smartest people in the world.

You *can* change. People in worse shape than you have succeeded, have found a new and far better way of living because they were sick and tired of being sick and tired and wanted something else. Do you want it too?

You have a choice. Make a decision.

Goals of This Workbook

Our previous experience in treating chemically dependent criminal offenders has shown that anyone who makes an honest effort to complete the exercises and practice the concepts can succeed.

The four goals of this criminal and addictive thinking program are to help you

1. learn how to think about your own thinking

2. learn that distorted, extreme thinking leads to distorted, extreme emotions and behavior

3. learn how to identify and stop old criminal and addictive thinking patterns before you act or react

4. replace unsuccessful patterns of thinking with rational choices that will, over time, change those old patterns and lead you to a happier, healthier, more free way of life

Facilitator Note
This module can be used concurrently with the *Drug & Alcohol Education* module. Using the two modules together will help to reinforce the connection between addiction and criminal behavior.

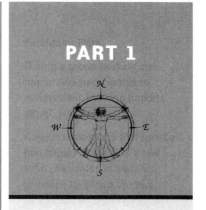
Criminal and Addiction History

The first step in creating a new thought map is to understand why you *need* a new map. To do that, you must recognize that you are where you are today because of your current map.

You have to identify the problem and take responsibility for it. As a criminal and addictive thinker, you most likely will first respond by saying, "I haven't got a problem. I'm fine."

You may deny that alcohol or other drugs are a problem for you. You may deny that you like the rush of excitement of doing forbidden things. You may even deny the terrible consequences of your criminal lifestyle and addiction, even though you are looking through bars and razor wire.

Addicts and criminals think and behave in many ways when using drugs or committing crimes. Some want to fight or argue; some feel sorry for themselves; while some blame others for their problems. Some go off by themselves, abandoning their family and friends. Others act out aggressively. Some criminals and addicts do all of this—and more! We'll learn more about the different types of criminal and addictive thinking patterns in parts 3 and 4.

**Changing these patterns
will be your map to
freedom and sobriety.**

EXERCISE **2** EXERCISE

Your Criminal History

The first step to honesty and recovery is admitting to and taking responsibility for your criminal past. List every crime you've been arrested and convicted for. Write the year of the offense after each listing.

For some of you, this will be a long list. If necessary, complete this exercise in a notebook. List your crimes in order, from your most recent all the way back to your first crime.

➤ Crime   Year

_____

_____

_____

_____

_____

_____

_____

_____

_____

_____

_____

_____

_____

_____

_____

_____

Facilitator Note
Emphasize that participants list only the crimes they've been convicted for. This will avoid future complications.

You have to identify the problem—and take responsibility for it.

➤ How much time have you spent locked up for these offenses?

_____ years   _____ months

➤ What is the longest time you have spent crime free?

_____ years   _____ months

➤ Now think about all the crimes you've committed that you never got caught for. How many crimes do you guess you've done that you were never arrested or convicted for?

_____

➤ Over the course of your life, how much time and energy have you spent thinking about ways to make illegal money—make a quick score—or do some other type of crime?

Check one.

☐   I have spent almost all my time and energy that way.

☐   I have spent much of my time and energy that way. *(50 percent or more)*

☐   I have spent some time and energy that way. *(less than 50 percent)*

☐   I have never spent time or energy thinking about crime.

➤ Look at the list of your crimes on page 15. Did they happen more and more often, or did they seem to go in "bursts" (a lot of crime followed by a cooling-off period followed by a lot of crime again)? What patterns do you see in your criminal activity throughout your life?

_____

_____

_____

_____

_____

_____

_____

➤ What crimes did you commit while under the influence of alcohol or other drugs?

_____

_____

_____

_____

Facilitator Note

The purpose of this part of the exercise is to help participants see the causal relationship between chemical use and committing certain crimes. In group, you may want to explore the types of crimes most likely to be committed under the influence and the types most likely to be committed when not using.

Be wary, however, of participants trying to duck accountability by blaming drug or alcohol use for their criminal behaviors. This is a common trap for therapists. Criminal thinking begins long before the commission of the particular crime. Chemical use may lower inhibitions or help increase impulsivity, but it is not a primary cause of criminal behavior. _Criminal thinking_ is the primary cause.

➤ What crimes did you commit while *not* under the influence of alcohol or other drugs?

_____

_____

_____

_____

_____

_____

➤ What crimes did you commit while trying to get alcohol or other drugs?

_____

_____

_____

_____

_____

_____

_____

➤ Did you ever switch to different types of crimes? (check one)

_____ Yes   _____ No

If so, why did you switch, and when?

_____

_____

_____

➤ Were most of your crimes committed on the spur of the moment, or did you think them through first? For example, did you ever steal just for the thrill of it? Give some examples of how you planned or didn't plan crimes from your own criminal history.

1. _____

_____

_____

_____

2. _____

_____

_____

3. _____

_____

_____

Were most of your crimes committed on the spur of the moment, or did you think them through first?

➤ List three reasons why you think your criminal behavior is out of control. Examples may include wanting to stop but doing it anyway, committing crimes even when you didn't care if you got caught, committing crime for the fun of it, and so on. In each of the three examples, describe the crime itself and how it seemed out of control.

1. _____

_____

_____

_____

2. _____

_____

_____

_____

3. _____

_____

_____

_____

➤ For you, what have been the five worst consequences of your criminal behavior?

1. _____

2. _____

3. _____

4. _____

5. _____

➤ For your family, friends, and victims, what have been the consequences of your criminal behavior?

1. _____

2. _____

3. _____

4. _____

5. _____

Facilitator Note

This portion of the exercise is designed to get participants to think about their criminal behavior and its impact on both themselves and others.

See the *Socialization* module for a more in-depth study of victim impact.

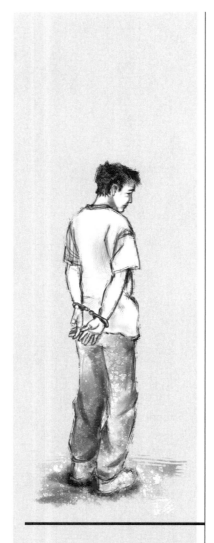

> Give five reasons why criminal behavior and a criminal lifestyle seemed attractive to you.

1. _____

_____

_____

2. _____

_____

_____

3. _____

_____

_____

4. _____

_____

_____

5. _____

_____

_____

What have been the worst consequences of your criminal behavior?

Your Addiction History

➤ Just as with your criminal history, the first step to honesty and recovery from your addiction is admitting your chemical history. List every type of drug you have used to get high, as far back as you can remember. After listing each drug, write the year you first used it and the year you most recently used it.

Again, for some of you, this will be a long list. If necessary, complete this exercise in a notebook. **Note:** List each drug only once. Don't list every single time you got high on the drug—just the first and most recent time you used it.

Drug	Year of first use	Year of most recent use
_____	_____	_____
_____	_____	_____
_____	_____	_____
_____	_____	_____
_____	_____	_____
_____	_____	_____
_____	_____	_____
_____	_____	_____
_____	_____	_____
_____	_____	_____

➤ What are your drugs of choice? Just before your most recent arrest, how much did you use of each in a typical week?

Drug	Amount used each week
1. _____	_____
2. _____	_____
3. _____	_____
4. _____	_____

➤ Did you ever have trouble concentrating because you day-dreamed about using alcohol or other drugs? (check one)

_____ Yes   _____ No

If so, how often did this happen? (circle one)

Rarely   Often   Constantly

➤ Did your use of alcohol or other drugs increase or decrease over time? If it increased, how? What time in your life was your use the heaviest?

_____

_____

_____

_____

Facilitator Note

Participants may tend to distort their report of their heaviest or lightest chemical usage by claiming they were "just getting it together" when they were arrested and incarcerated. It is highly unlikely that this is, in fact, the case. If you get this response, you may want to ask why they were "getting it together" at this time, since people rarely change behaviors that are working for them.

➤ Give five reasons why using alcohol or other drugs seemed attractive to you.

1. _____

2. _____

3. _____

4. _____

5. _____

Did you ever switch from one drug to another? (check one)

_____ Yes   _____ No

➤ Why or why not?

_____

_____

_____

_____

_____

_____

_____

Facilitator Note

Answers might include
• "escaping reality,"
• "everyone else was doing it,"
• "it felt good," or
• "it helped me cope with all that was going on."

You might even get answers saying how cool it looked on television or in the movies.

Facilitator Note
This is known as the
"geographical cure."

➤ Did you ever move to another neighborhood, city, or state to escape the consequences of your alcohol or other drug use or to "get a fresh start"? Explain.

_____

_____

_____

➤ Did you hide your drug of choice? If so, why and from whom? How did you protect your supply?

_____

_____

_____

Blackout

A *blackout* is when a person under the influence of alcohol or other drugs continues to function but has no memory afterward of what happened. A blackout is not passing out; it is a period of time when you cannot recall what happened.

➤ Have you ever *blacked out* or overdosed taking drugs or drinking? List examples.

_____

_____

_____

_____

_____

_____

➤ List four examples of abuse that you committed while you were high. The types of abuse are physical, emotional, verbal, and sexual.

Facilitator Note

To help participants recall these abusive events, you may refer them back to exercise 2 on page 14.

1. _____

   _____

   _____

2. _____

   _____

   _____

3. _____

   _____

   _____

4. _____

   _____

   _____

➤ Have you ever felt bad about things you did while you were high? Explain.

_____

_____

_____

Facilitator Note

You may choose to ask them if their current incarceration involved the use of alcohol or other drugs.

➤ List five reasons why you think your addiction is out of control. Examples may include wanting to stop but using anyway, seeking out drugs even though you knew it was dangerous, committing crimes only because you needed to get high, and so on. Describe each incident and how it seemed out of control.

1. _____

_____

_____

2. _____

_____

_____

3. _____

_____

_____

4. _____

_____

_____

5. _____

_____

_____

➤ For you, what have been the five worst consequences of your use of alcohol or other drugs?

1. _____

_____

Facilitator Note
Incarceration should be one of the first consequences listed here. If it's not listed, ask them why and be prepared to challenge them on this.

2. _____

_____

3. _____

_____

4. _____

_____

5. _____

_____

➤ For your family and friends, what have been the consequences of your use of alcohol or other drugs?

What have been the consequences of your use of alcohol or other drugs?

1. _____

_____

2. _____

_____

3. _____

_____

4. _____

_____

5. _____

_____

➤ Have you ever promised or tried to stop using alcohol or other drugs? Explain.

_____

_____

_____

Facilitator Note
You may wish to ask whether their longer stretches of sobriety coincide with being incarcerated or other potential interruptions of supply.

➤ What is the longest time you have been sober (not used alcohol or other drugs) since you started using?

_____

➤ Why did you try to sober up?

_____

_____

➤ Why did you start using again?

_____

_____

Facilitator Note
You may wish to ask participants if they sought any form
of outside help (e.g., self-help
groups, religious counseling,
psychological therapy) during
the period of relative sobriety.

➤ Have you ever been in drug or alcohol treatment before?
List each place of treatment, the year you entered, and
whether you were forced to enter or you entered of your
own free will. List your treatments in order, from your
most recent back to your first treatment. State whether
you completed them.

Facilitator Note
Virtually no criminal-addict
enters treatment voluntarily.
If a participant claims otherwise, it is probably worth
challenging in group.

Treatment place	Year	Forced?	Completed?
_____	_____	_____	_____
_____	_____	_____	_____
_____	_____	_____	_____
_____	_____	_____	_____
_____	_____	_____	_____
_____	_____	_____	_____
_____	_____	_____	_____
_____	_____	_____	_____
_____	_____	_____	_____
_____	_____	_____	_____

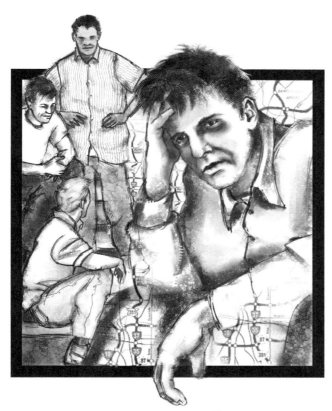

Becoming Aware of Your Inner Maps

*We look at the world **through** our maps.*
*We seldom stop to look **at** our maps.*

The first step to changing your thinking is to become aware of your thinking patterns. In order to "think about your thinking," you must first stop and identify your thoughts. Over time, you will see a pattern.

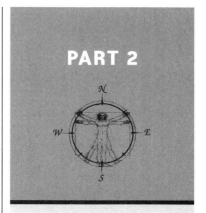

PART 2

A NEW DIRECTION

A Cognitive-Behavioral Treatment Curriculum

Facilitator Note
This material may be best presented in a lecture format with the opportunity for questions and answers. The goal is for participants to achieve some measure of understanding of the cognitive model before going on to part 3.

You may want to use a chalkboard or overhead projector to show the four graphic representations of the cognitive model to help them visualize how it works. These can be found in figures 4, 5, 6, and 7 on pages 34, 35, 43, and 44 in this section.

Keep in mind that we take our thinking for granted—much of it is "automatic" because we believe "that's just the way things are." Because of this, we tend to get thoughts mixed up with feelings, beliefs, and attitudes. To begin to sort it all out, we need to understand how thinking works.

Noticing Your Thoughts

Most thoughts happen in response to some sort of event. The event may be someone bumping into you, the smell of good food, your favorite team scoring a touchdown, or your partner yelling at you. After an event, some thoughts arise right away. Other thoughts may come later, especially if the event is seen as negative. Almost always, some sort of behavior will result from these thoughts. This is how it works:

Figure 4

The event leads to the thoughts. The thoughts cause the behavior.

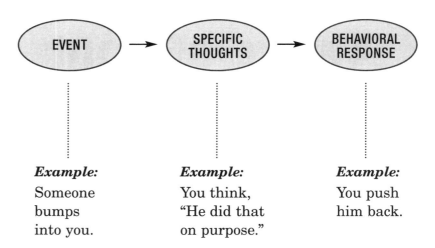

Example:
Someone bumps into you.

Example:
You think, "He did that on purpose."

Example:
You push him back.

Often, this happens so quickly you don't even notice your thoughts. You may believe the behavior results directly from the event. This is simply not true.

Your behaviors are <u>always</u> the result of your thinking, whether you're fully aware of your thoughts or not.

This is very important: Your behavior never bypasses your brain. The event triggers specific thoughts, which lead to your actions (behaviors).

Figure 5

The event **does not** lead directly to the behavior. There are **always** thoughts that arise first, even if you are not fully aware of them.

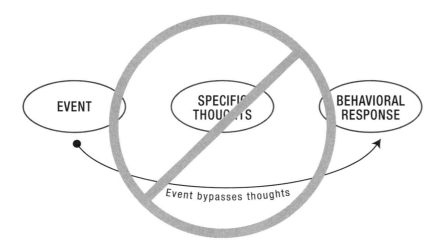

Your behavior NEVER bypasses your brain.

4a.
Noticing Thoughts

Imagine that you are in your apartment in a large apartment building. It's 11 at night. You're wide awake and feeling pretty good. You're playing your stereo loud—your favorite CD—and you're really enjoying it. There's a knock at your door. You open it to see a guy standing there with a frown on his face. It's obvious that he's upset.

"Man, could you turn it down? The music is coming right through the walls, and I'm trying to sleep. I've got to work tomorrow."

You think, "Who is this guy to tell me what to do in my own apartment?" You feel the blood rushing to your face, feel the anger starting to build. You pause. Then you let him have it:

"F—— you. This is my place. I pay the rent here. You think I don't work? You're f——ing with the wrong guy, buddy. Get the hell out of here."

As you speak, you lean forward and puff out your chest. Your fingers close into a fist and open and close again. You glare at the man, who has taken a half-step back, stunned. You wait a moment for your words to sink in. You slam the door in his face and go back to your stereo. You turn the volume up another notch and sit down on your couch. Your good mood is now long gone. You are fuming. Your thoughts continue to spin. You want a drink (or a fix or a joint), and you want it now. You start thinking about where and how to get one.

Facilitator Note

Ideally, participants should be able to complete this exercise on their own. If reading level is an issue, you may ask participants to work in teams of two. They can read each page out loud together and then discuss it.

The purpose of this exercise is to identify their distorted views of the event. Often, they confuse the actual event with their emotion surrounding the event.

It's important that the participants complete this exercise and fully understand it since exercises 5 and 7 refer back to this exercise.

What just happened? Why did it happen? Did it have to happen the way it did?

The details aren't important: It's the thinking and response we're concerned with. It doesn't matter whether you think you would respond like this or not. The point is, many criminals and addicts *would* think and react this way, and the chances are good you might, too. It's fairly predictable because it's part of a thinking pattern common to many criminals and addicts.

This pattern of thinking makes up your personal thought map. As you'll see later, your personal thought map isn't unique. It represents a thinking pattern you share with most other addicts and criminals.

➤ What thoughts might be going through your head after the man tells you to turn down your music? List them below.

EXAMPLE:

"Nobody can tell me what to do in my own apartment."

1. _____

   _____

2. _____

   _____

3. _____

   _____

➤ You may have many other thoughts after you slam the door. Imagine yourself in the situation again and list three more possible thoughts.

EXAMPLE:

"I'm minding my own business. Why doesn't he mind his?"

1. _____

_____

2. _____

_____

3. _____

_____

■ ■ ■

4b.
Noticing Thoughts

Imagine yourself in another situation.

It's at night and you're in your cell during free time. A female officer approaches your cell and says, "You need to turn down the radio. It's too loud. I've talked to you about this before—next time I'm writing you up."

You think, among other things: "F——ing b——. She's had it in for me since I got here. That's not loud! The guy next door plays his louder and she never says anything to him. I can't believe that b—— is telling me to turn down my s—— in my house. She's on a power trip."

At first you say nothing. You pause and glare at her. Then you say, "It's not that loud. Other guys play it just as loud." She tells you again that you must turn down the music. You mutter something she can't hear, roll your eyes, and walk over and turn the radio down.

➤ What other thoughts might go through your head? List them.

1. _____

_____

2. _____

_____

3. _____

_____

➤ Why would you say some thoughts out loud but not others?

_____

_____

_____

_____

_____

■ ■ ■

What thoughts go through your head when someone confronts you?

4c.
Noticing Thoughts

Imagine this: You're walking in the yard and another inmate, someone you don't know, brushes up against you as he passes by.

➤ What thoughts arise for you *right now* as you think about this happening to you? Write down as many as you can. If necessary, complete this exercise in a notebook.

1. _____

   _____

2. _____

   _____

3. _____

   _____

4. _____

   _____

5. _____

   _____

Facilitator Note

It's important that the participants complete this exercise and fully understand it since exercises 5 and 7 refer back to this exercise.

Reporting Events

The event is the thing that happened that led to the thoughts, feelings, and behavior. Go back and reread the situations described in exercise 4a, exercise 4b, and exercise 4c. Three separate events took place. List and describe the event in each of the three situations.

➤ Exercise 4a event:

_____

_____

_____

➤ Exercise 4b event:

_____

_____

_____

➤ Exercise 4c event:

_____

_____

_____

With your group, talk about your report of the three events. Did you actually report just the events, or did you give your judgment and feelings about the events?

Facilitator Note

If participants resist rewriting the events here, you may choose to do this exercise in a group setting. Ask participants to refer to the stories in exercises 4a, 4b, and 4c and to write them in their own words.

Then ask for two or three volunteers to read their versions of the events. It is likely that at least one of them will have a distorted version. This will help normalize their tendency to interpret and report incidents in a biased or distorted way.

Reporting Events and Noticing Thoughts

Facilitator Note

You will need to help participants distinguish between the event and a judgment, interpretation, or elaboration of the event. The event should be a succinct, dispassionate report. A wordy explanation is usually an attempt to distort and exploit the truth of what happened to suit one's own interests.

One common error in reporting events involves mistaking the event for an emotional snap judgment of it; e.g., "He dissed me" rather than "He rolled his eyes in response to what I was saying."

A common error in reporting thoughts is the tendency to confuse emotions with thoughts.

Now think about an event that actually happened to you either yesterday or today. It doesn't matter whether it made you feel good, bad, or nothing at all. All we're concerned about is learning to notice and clearly identify your thoughts. In writing down the event, just report the facts of what happened. For instance, "I was disrespected" is not an event; it's an *interpretation* or judgment of an event. Your identification of the event should be a simple description of what happened. In other words, try to step outside yourself in reporting the event.

➤ What was the event?

_____

_____

➤ What were your thoughts in response to this event?

_____

_____

_____

_____

_____

_____

Noticing Your Feelings

We've learned to identify events. These events lead to thoughts, and thoughts result in behavior. Feelings, or emotions, also result from specific thoughts about the event. How you think affects your feelings.

Facilitator Note

Figures 6 and 7 are used to illustrate important concepts in this curriculum. It is critical that participants understand these concepts.

As noted earlier, you may want to write this on a chalkboard or overhead projector to aid in the comprehension of the material.

Figure 6

Feelings also result from thoughts.

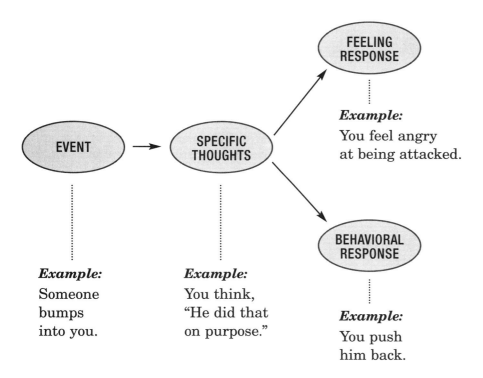

Example:
Someone bumps into you.

Example:
You think, "He did that on purpose."

Example:
You feel angry at being attacked.

Example:
You push him back.

Again, your reaction to an event happens so quickly that you often don't notice your thoughts. Just as the behavior seems to result directly from the event, it may also seem that feelings arise from the event. This is also not true.

Your behaviors and your feelings are always the result of your thinking, whether you're fully aware of your thoughts or not.

An event triggers specific thoughts, which lead to both your feelings and your actions (behaviors).

Figure 7

Feelings **do not** result from events.
Feelings come out of the **thoughts** that arise from the event.

Behaviors **do not** result from feelings.
Behaviors come out of the **thoughts** that arise from the event

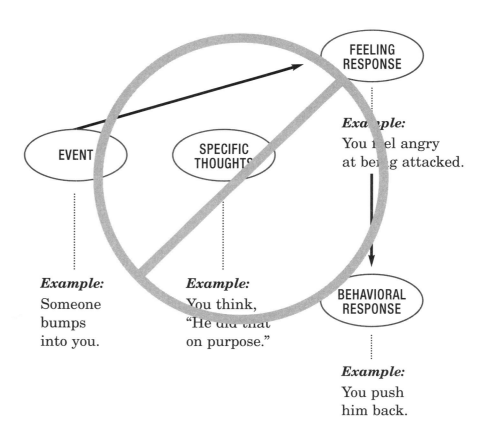

FEELING RESPONSE

Example:
You feel angry at being attacked.

EVENT

SPECIFIC THOUGHTS

BEHAVIORAL RESPONSE

Example:
Someone bumps into you.

Example:
You think, "He did that on purpose."

Example:
You push him back.

For example, a man who has hit his wife may say, "She made me angry and I just snapped." This suggests that he believes she was responsible for his feelings (anger) and the feelings directly caused the behavior (he "snapped" and became violent). This is not the case. If he looked more closely, he'd find that his thoughts led to the violent behavior. Some of his thoughts may have been

- "How dare she talk back to me."

- "This is my house. I'm the man here."

- "She's been on my case all day."

- "She was asking for it."

Emotions do have a role to play with thoughts. When you're emotionally upset, you are more likely to have *a lot* of negative thoughts. These thoughts may lead to negative behaviors.

 EXERCISE 7 EXERCISE

Noticing Feeling Responses to Thoughts

What are feelings? To figure it out, let's look at the example of the event in exercise 4a, the man at your door telling you to turn down your stereo. Choose two of the thoughts you listed in exercise 4a as responses to that event. Then list two possible feeling responses to each thought.

EXAMPLE:

Specific thought	Possible feeling responses
"Nobody tells me what to do in my apartment."	*"I'm angry that the good got interrupted."*
	"I feel embarrassed about being caught by surprise."

Facilitator Note
Cognitive researchers differ on how to view the primacy of feelings and thoughts in the cognitive-behavioral model. It is our position that feelings powerfully reinforce thoughts and behaviors and therefore play a major role in creating thinking and behavior patterns. In the treatment of criminal offenders, however, we argue that although feelings are important in any cognitive treatment model, remediation of behavior is the critical problem. We believe a thinking → behavior causality should be emphasized as the most direct route toward helping offenders make the fundamental cognitive changes required to alter behavior.

➤ **Specific thought**

_____

_____

_____

Possible feeling responses

1. _____

_____

_____

2. _____

_____

_____

➤ **Specific thought**

_____

_____

_____

Possible feeling responses

1. _____

_____

_____

2. _____

_____

_____

A wide range of feelings could result from the thoughts a person has in response to any event. Some feelings are pleasant or enjoyable ("I feel happy about that"), and some are unpleasant and disturbing ("That makes me feel really angry"). There are also many types of feelings that would fall between those two opposites. In fact, in the English language, there are about two thousand single words, not counting longer phrases or even slang words, that could complete the sentence "I feel _____."

One of the first steps in identifying, understanding, and recognizing feelings in yourself and others is learning how to give names to your emotions. The same emotion can have several names depending on whether the feeling is mild or more intense.

Emotion	Mild	Moderate	Extreme
Sad	disappointed	gloomy	devastated
Afraid	nervous	scared	terrified
Desire	wish	want	crave
Disgusted	dislike	contempt	revulsion
Angry	annoyed	indignant	furious
Guilty	regretful	sorry	self-hating
Shamed	embarrassed	unworthy	humiliated

Thinking Patterns

Figure 6 showed how feelings and behaviors result from the specific thoughts that arise from the event. When you have the same types of thoughts over and over, you create *thinking patterns*.

Thinking patterns are habits of thinking and responding that become automatic. As you repeat these patterns over time, you begin to believe that these thinking patterns are absolute reality: "That's just the way I am," you may tell yourself (and others). But you are wrong. Thinking patterns are not "just the way you are." They are "just the way *you have come to believe you are.*" The problem is, once your thinking responses are automatic, you don't question whether those thoughts are the most effective way to deal with things.

Facilitator Note

In his book *Words for Our Feelings,* psychotherapist Dan Jones points out that to identify more clearly our emotional feeling responses, we can eliminate the following categories of words that are part feeling words and part behavior words:

- Words that are more descriptive of the stimulus (event) than the feeling response, such as "I feel threatened."
- Words that better describe an action to follow the feeling, such as "I feel promiscuous."
- Words that describe thinking states rather than feeling states, such as "I feel clever" or "I feel confused."

In addition, nonspecific feeling words—*terrific, bad, crummy, great*—aren't particularly helpful in articulating feeling responses; they are merely variants of "I feel good (or bad)."

(continued on page 48)

> **Thinking Patterns**
>
> *Thinking patterns* are habits of thinking and responding that become automatic.

Facilitator Note
(continued from page 47)

Feeling words for physical sensations—*energetic*— or altered states—*high*— obviously have their descriptive value, but they are not emotional feeling responses.

If we narrow the list to only those feeling words that describe emotional states, we find there are seven basic categories:

1. Sadness: words such as *disappointed* (mild sadness) to *desolate* (extreme sadness)
2. Fear: *uneasy* (mild) to *terrified* (extreme)
3. Desire: *wishful* (mild) to *insatiable* (extreme)
4. Aversion: *dislike* (mild) to *loathing* (extreme)
5. Anger: *irritated* (mild) to *raging* (extreme)
6. Guilt: *sheepish* (mild) to *self-hatred* (extreme)
7. Shame: *embarrassed* (mild) to *humiliated* (extreme)*

One way of distinguishing between guilt and shame: guilt is feeling bad about what you did, and shame is feeling bad about what you *are*.

* Dan Jones, *Words for Our Feelings: A Concise and Practical Guide to the Names for the Various Moods, Emotions, Sensations, and Feelings* (Austin, Texas: Mandala Books, 1992), pp. 9–23.

What thoughts do you have when you think about entering a chemical dependency treatment program? Positive thoughts? Chances are, they are not. Very few people have happy associations with mandatory drug or alcohol treatment. It is important to understand, however, that this is not "just the way things are."

The thought "having to complete treatment is bad luck," like every other thought, is a choice.

You could just as easily choose to think that being in treatment is good luck.

Patterns of thinking aren't <u>given</u> to us; they're <u>learned and created</u> by us over time.

These patterns of thought are your map of the world: They decide what the world looks like to you and where you choose to go and what you decide to do, day in and day out. If your map is faulty, you're going to get lost. You're going to experience a lot of conflict with others and society. By following faulty mental maps: (a) you broke the law and ended up with the negative social consequences and (b) felt discontented and miserable a lot of the time. If you follow those faulty maps over and over again, you'll probably end up incarcerated and miserable over and over again—and that's insane.

Insanity is doing the same thing over and over and expecting different results.

Where Are You Going?

➤ When you were a child, you probably didn't tell adults, "I want to be a criminal and an addict when I grow up." What did you want to be when you were younger?

_____

_____

_____

➤ What kind of life do you want to lead? Be realistic—skip the "sitting around the pool of my mansion" fantasy. Try to imagine a real living situation you would like to achieve.

_____

_____

_____

_____

Facilitator Note

You may need to help participants construct realistic goals. They will tend either to have no goals or to engage in extreme magical thinking. If your participants struggle with this part of exercise 8, you may want to narrow the question and ask what kind of life they want within the first six months following release.

➤ What parts of your personal mental map lead you away from responsible goals?

_____

_____

_____

_____

Changing Your Flawed Thought Map

Your personal thought map may be flawed in three ways:

1. It was created in the first place, and continues to be revised and adapted, based on thinking distortions.

2. It is made up of particular habits of thinking called **criminal and addictive thinking patterns.**

3. It is supported by **core beliefs,** basic assumptions you have made about yourself, others, and the world that may be in conflict with the facts.

Thinking distortions aren't about *what* you think, but rather *how* you think. To change your faulty thought map, you are first going to have to begin to understand and change *how you think*.

Criminal and addictive thinking patterns are types of inaccurate thoughts that you have used repeatedly and acted on over the course of your life. They are categories of thoughts that are almost guaranteed to lead you into criminal behavior and drug or alcohol use. Let's take a closer look at these two kinds of thinking patterns.

Criminal thinking patterns are common to all criminals. Not every criminal has every single criminal thinking pattern, but every criminal has *many* and probably *most* of them. Criminal thinking patterns are the ways of thinking that say it is all right for you to violate others or the property of others.

Examples of typical criminal thinking patterns are

- "I found myself in a situation."
- "I'd rather be doing time than be straight like you."
- "I punched him because he had no right to look at me that way."

Because you are addicted to alcohol or other drugs, your thought map is also filled with *addictive thinking patterns*. Addictive thinking patterns are common to all addicts, though not every addict has every single one. Addictive thinking patterns overlap a great deal with criminal thinking patterns, and the two reinforce and drive each other. Addictive thinking patterns are those ways of thinking that say continuing to use alcohol or other drugs is okay no matter what you have to do to make that happen and no matter what the consequences are to yourself or others.

Examples of typical addictive thinking patterns are

- "I can quit whenever I want."
- "My problem isn't drinking; it's my wife's nagging."
- "Nothing ever works out. I deserve to get high."

Core beliefs are assumptions you have made and accepted as true about yourself, others, and the world. They are the most hidden part of your personal thought map. In a way, core beliefs are like the layers of rocks beneath the surface of the land.

Figure 8

A map doesn't show what the country looks like deep beneath the earth's surface.

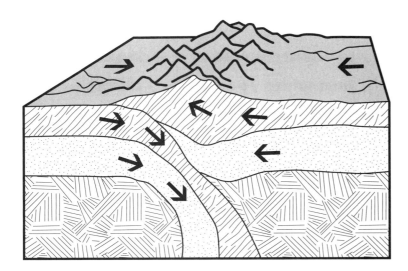

A map of a country will show what the surface of the country looks like: where the roads, rivers, mountains, and so on are located. But beneath the surface are layers of rock and minerals built up and worn down and shifted around over millions of years by oceans, glaciers, volcanoes, earthquakes, wind, and other forces. A map doesn't show what the country looks like deep beneath the earth's surface. It shows what the surface looks like. Your core beliefs are the deep, unseen part of your mental map. They determine which common thinking distortions (*how* you think) and criminal and addictive thinking patterns (*what* you think) are on your personal thought map.

Here are some examples of core beliefs:

- "I'm not responsible to anybody or anything."
- "Most people are suckers."
- "Life is supposed to be fair."

To build a life free of criminal behavior and alcohol or other drug use, you need to make some choices to fix your personal thought map. You will need to change your map so that it more accurately represents reality and no longer leads you back to incarceration, broken relationships, poor health, and so on.

Your core beliefs are the deep, unseen part of your mental map.

The first step in fixing your thought map is to identify where it is inaccurate and what you need to change. To do that, you have to be able to think about your thinking.

How to Fill Out a Thinking Report

A Thinking Report is a way for you to practice thinking about your thinking, your core beliefs, and your behavior so you can change them. Thinking about their thinking is a skill that successful people have developed to some degree and that unsuccessful people have developed only slightly or not at all.

Remember, negative thoughts lead to negative behaviors, which lead to negative consequences. Positive, practical thoughts lead to alternative behaviors, which either lead to positive consequences or, at the very least, help to avoid negative consequences.

Thinking Reports are a very important tool in helping you learn how to read your own inner map. They will help you to

1. gradually become *aware* of your own thinking, and

2. learn how to start *thinking* about your own thinking.

Knowing how to think about your own thinking is the most important basic skill you need to create a new, successful thought map.

There are seven main parts to the Thinking Report. They are

1. The **Event**—what exactly happened to begin the chain of thoughts, feelings, and behaviors or potential behaviors.

2. Your **Thoughts**—what popped into your mind when the event occurred.

3. Your **Feelings**—the emotions or other sensations that resulted from your thoughts about the event.

4. Your **Behavior**—your actions in response to the event as directed by your thoughts and reinforced by your feelings.

Facilitator Note

Thinking Reports will be discussed here. Emphasize that a Thinking Report is an important tool for behavior change. Extra copies of thinking reports can be found on pages 302–303 of this workbook. Unlike other material in this workbook, these Thinking Reports may be duplicated without permission from the publisher.

You may choose to show the *Thinking About Your Thinking, Part I* video (included with this module) that examines individual components of the Thinking Report during an actual group session. It includes tips on taking responsibility for your actions and takes a hard look at criminal thinking errors. In the *Thinking About Your Thinking, Part 2* video (included with this module), there are eight scenarios/role plays. you may choose to show portions of this video throughout this module. These role plays are ideal for teaching participants how to effectively work through Thinking Reports. After each scenario is played, there is an opportunity to pause and have the participants complete Thinking Reports. Scenarios include: a random cell shakedown, dealing with having a bad day, cutting in line to use the microwave, confronting others, resolving conflicts, refusing to get involved in illegal activities, resolving issues on the basketball court, and dealing with family members.

5. Your **Core Beliefs**—the assumptions you make about the world, others, and yourself.

6. Possible **Alternative Thoughts**—healthier thoughts that are different from your first, automatic thoughts and that could lead to a more positive outcome.

7. Possible **Alternative Behaviors**—what you could do based on your alternative thoughts.

Three remaining sections of the Thinking Report—Thinking distortions, Thinking patterns, and tactics—will be discussed in sections 3, 4, and 6 of these workbooks. Leave these sections blank for now.

The Thinking Reports looks like this.

Facilitator Note

Additional Thinking Reports can be found in the back of the workbook on pages 302–303.

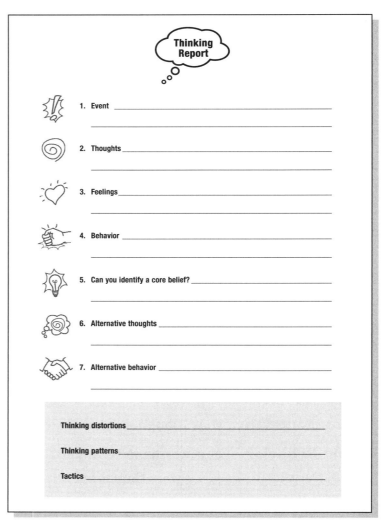

Event

The event is the situation that led to your negative thoughts. The event does not include your responses to the situation—your thoughts, feelings, and behavior regarding what happened. It is simply the thing that happened itself. Your thoughts arise in *response* to the event.

When you fill out a Thinking Report, briefly describe just the facts of what happened—the who, what, when, and where of the situation—as completely as you can. Remember to try to tell the story of the event as someone else who saw the event would describe it.

EXAMPLE:

*You are sitting down to eat your lunch. A peer walks up to you and says, "You're sitting in my chair. Get out **now.**" Then he stares at you.*

This is an accurate report of the event	These are *not* accurate reports of the event
I sat down to lunch and this guy tells me I'm in his seat. Then he starts mean mugging and telling me to move.	This dude was trying to make me look like a punk during lunch. *(This is a judgment **about** the event.)*
	I told this guy trying to jack my seat at lunch that he had me confused with someone who gave a s—— about what he thinks. *(This is a judgment about and a behavior response to the event.)*

Thoughts

Thoughts are the automatic notions or images you have at the time of the event. To say that these notions, or thoughts, are automatic means they do not arise from a calm process of reasoning but rather just seem to "pop" into your head in the moment.

For this part of the Thinking Report, you list the main thought or thoughts you had at the time of the event.

EXAMPLE:

These are possible (automatic) thoughts

I don't see his name on the bench. What's he trying pull?

Who is this guy? Who's he hanging with?

This dude's disrespecting me, trying to back me down.

F—— you. Who do you think you are?

Feelings

Feelings are the emotions that arise at the time of the event. These emotions may be sad, anxious, angry, pleased, relieved, frightened, or other such feelings. (For more information on feelings, see pages 45–47.) Though these feelings seem to pop up separately from the automatic thoughts you had, in reality, they are the *result* of those thoughts.

In your Thinking Report, list the feelings that you had at the time of the event. Try to determine how intense each feeling was—mild, fairly intense, very intense, or overwhelming.

EXAMPLE:

These are possible feelings

Angry *(very intense)*	Humiliated *(fairly intense)*
Fearful *(intense)*	Nervous *(mild)*

These are *not* feelings

I'll kick his ass.
(This is a thought about how you will respond.)

Others might think I'm a chump if I don't do something.
(This is an automatic thought expressing a fear of humiliation.)

Behavior

The behavior is what you say or do in response to the event. It is the direct result of the negative automatic thoughts you listed. Often the behavior will be a criminal or addictive *tactic*—a strategy you have learned to try to get the results that you think you want. (See part 6, Learning to Think about Your Behavior, pages 263–299.) Behavior occurs after the thinking stage. It is *action*. Sometimes it will be something you say; sometimes it will be a physical act; sometimes it will be both.

Describe your behavior in your Thinking Report.

EXAMPLE:

This could be the behavior	**This is *not* the behavior**
I told him, "Get lost, punk. I'm sitting here now." Then I stood up and stared him down.	I set him straight—let him know who he was messing with. *(This is an interpretation of the behavior, a judgment thought about the behavior after the act had been completed.)*

Your behavior is what you say or do in response to an event.

Core Beliefs

Core beliefs are the basic assumptions we make about the world, others, and ourselves. They make up what we assume to be true about reality and our own self-identity. Core beliefs are formed in childhood as a result of our experiences of the world and are so automatic that we usually aren't even aware of them unless we stop to think carefully.

The main thing to understand about core beliefs is that they are the thoughts behind our thoughts—the things we hold to be true. Our automatic thoughts come out of these beliefs. (Core beliefs are explained more completely on pages 51–52 and in part 4 of these workbooks.)

To fill out a Thinking Report, you list one or more core belief. Remember, they are the thoughts *behind* the automatic thoughts you've already listed.

EXAMPLE:

These are possible core beliefs	These are *not* core beliefs
People will always take advantage of you if you let them, especially behind bars.	I really hate that SOB. *(This is a thought showing awareness of a feeling.)*
I'm better than him; I deserve respect.	He must think I'm weak. *(This is an automatic response thought.)*
It's a dog-eat-dog world.	
If I don't watch out for myself, no one will.	

Facilitator Note

Alternative Thoughts

Alternative thoughts are the thoughts you *could choose* that would challenge your automatic thoughts. Interrupting your automatic negative thoughts gives you a chance to choose a different behavior that you can use over the long haul. Alternative thoughts are a way of mentally stepping out of the thoughts and emotions of the moment and not letting them lead to negative behavior.

Alternative thoughts ask questions such as

- How important is it really?

- How much is it going to cost me in the long term?

- How will I feel afterward if I do what I'm thinking of doing and then get hit with consequences?

Since you really have control over only your own thoughts and behaviors, coming up with alternative thoughts that help you avoid negative consequences is an example of true control—*self*-control.

EXAMPLE:

These are possible alternative thoughts

It's not worth going to seg over or getting kicked out of treatment.

This will blow by if I don't make a show of it.

What do I care where I sit? It's no big deal.

Alternative Behavior

The alternative behavior is the logical result of the alternative thoughts. An alternative behavior represents a different way of reacting (or not reacting), one that is in your long-term best interests. Alternative behavior is either new behavior, refraining from (*not* doing) some old behavior, or both.

EXAMPLE:

These are possible alternative behaviors

Say nothing and go sit somewhere else.

Tell him calmly, "I was sitting here. There are plenty of seats." And then go back to eating.

If the dude gets more threatening, go sit somewhere else and bring it up in group later.

At the bottom of the Thinking Report form are spaces for Thinking patterns, Thinking distortions, and Tactics. After you've completed parts 3, 4, and 6 of these workbooks, you'll be able to fill out those sections, too. For now, just concentrate on the main parts of the Thinking Report.

Remember: The purpose of Thinking Reports is to help you change your thinking and behaviors so that you can

- stay chemical free
- stay crime free
- become a better person in society

Choose situations for Thinking Reports that challenge you, that are difficult, that make you uncomfortable. Often they are the situations that will teach you new ways of thinking and living.

An alternative behavior represents a different way of reacting.

Facilitator Note

From this point on, Thinking Reports should become an essential part of the participant's activities with this module. It is recommended that participants do a minimum of three Thinking Reports per week; one every day is optimal.

9a.
Completing a Thinking Report

➤ Choose an incident that upset or bothered you either today or yesterday and report on what the *event* was, what *thoughts* you had in response to it, and the *feelings* that arose from those thoughts. Report also what you did—your *behavior*—as a result of those thoughts. Then try to figure out the *core belief* you have that may have led you to those thoughts. And finally, try to imagine *alternative thoughts* that could lead to *alternative behaviors* that wouldn't cause problems for you.

The Thinking Report can be found on page 62.

When you complete the report, ask for feedback from your therapist or group.

■ ■ ■

9b.
Completing a Thinking Report

➤ Do a new Thinking Report describing the same event you used in exercise 9a, but this time use the feedback you received from your therapist or group. Again, just do the seven main parts for now.

The Thinking Report can be found on page 63.

■

Facilitator Note

A sample thinking report including facilitator feedback is shown on page 64.

Facilitator Note

During a group session, ask one or two participants to review their Thinking Reports aloud.

Keep in mind that a therapeutic community that offers a low ratio of inmates to therapist, provides for group therapy several times weekly, and is supported by psychological services is a "safe" environment for inmate participants to explore issues relating to physical abuse, sexual abuse, abandonment, and family issues in childhood.

In contrast, large psycho-educational programs, with limited therapist-client interactions and few psychological services available should take great care in addressing issues that may cause the inmate to be overwhelmed and unsafe in the general population.

After participants read the Thinking Reports aloud, the reports are critiqued by the therapist and the peers in the group. At first, participants should only be asked to fill in the Event, Thoughts, Feelings, Behavior, and Core Belief portions of the Thinking Report, although it is recommended that they also start identifying Alternative Thoughts and Alternative Behaviors as early as possible. As other parts of the Thinking Report are covered in the workbook (Thinking Distortions, Thinking Patterns, and Tactics), participants should be asked to start identifying them as well.

Thinking Report

1. **Event** _____

   _____

2. **Thoughts** _____

   _____

3. **Feelings** _____

   _____

4. **Behavior** _____

   _____

5. **Can you identify a core belief?** _____

   _____

6. **Alternative thoughts** _____

   _____

7. **Alternative behavior** _____

   _____

Thinking distortions _____

Thinking patterns _____

Tactics _____

Thinking Report for Exercise 9b

Thinking Report

1. **Event** _____
   _____

2. **Thoughts** _____
   _____

3. **Feelings** _____
   _____

4. **Behavior** _____
   _____

5. **Can you identify a core belief?** _____
   _____

6. **Alternative thoughts** _____
   _____

7. **Alternative behavior** _____
   _____

Thinking distortions _____

Thinking patterns _____

Tactics _____

Sample Thinking Report with facilitator comments.

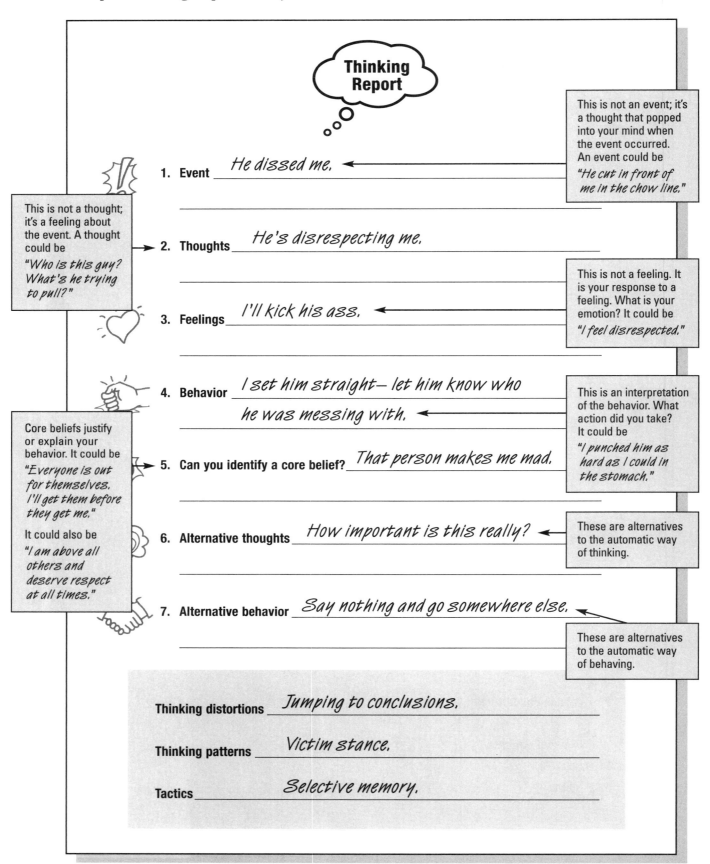

Thinking Report

1. **Event** _He dissed me._

   This is not an event; it's a thought that popped into your mind when the event occurred. An event could be *"He cut in front of me in the chow line."*

   This is not a thought; it's a feeling about the event. A thought could be *"Who is this guy? What's he trying to pull?"*

2. **Thoughts** _He's disrespecting me._

   This is not a feeling. It is your response to a feeling. What is your emotion? It could be *"I feel disrespected."*

3. **Feelings** _I'll kick his ass._

4. **Behavior** _I set him straight— let him know who he was messing with._

   This is an interpretation of the behavior. What action did you take? It could be *"I punched him as hard as I could in the stomach."*

   Core beliefs justify or explain your behavior. It could be *"Everyone is out for themselves. I'll get them before they get me."* It could also be *"I am above all others and deserve respect at all times."*

5. **Can you identify a core belief?** _That person makes me mad._

6. **Alternative thoughts** _How important is this really?_

   These are alternatives to the automatic way of thinking.

7. **Alternative behavior** _Say nothing and go somewhere else._

   These are alternatives to the automatic way of behaving.

Thinking distortions _Jumping to conclusions._

Thinking patterns _Victim stance._

Tactics _Selective memory._

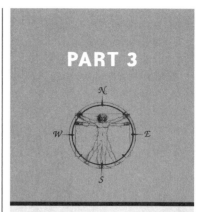

Learning to Think about Your Thinking

THINKING DISTORTIONS AND CRIMINAL THINKING PATTERNS

Now that you've come to understand how your inner thought maps lead you to act and feel the way you do, it's time to look closer at your thinking habits. How and what you think is what makes up your thought maps, so to change those maps, you need to learn how to change your thinking.

Facilitator Note

Suggest that as participants work through part 3, they circle any terms or descriptions that strike them as particularly accurate about themselves.

Some Basic Human Thinking Distortions

Thinking distortions are consistently inaccurate and biased ways that people use to look at themselves, others, and the world. Thinking distortions lead to thoughts and beliefs that may sound good on the surface or maybe have some slight truth to them.

But thinking distortions misrepresent or distort reality so that your mental map becomes faulty. The result is a self-serving mental map of reality that you use to rationalize and justify your criminal and addictive behavior. Thinking distortions are about *how* you think rather than *what* you think. As you will see, distortions in *how* you think can lead to distorted thoughts, distorted behaviors (criminality, irresponsibility), and distressing emotional and psychological conditions (extreme anxiety, rage, depression).

All people, not just criminals, use thinking distortions to some degree. These distortions are an almost automatic way of thinking. Often they are not obvious to the person using them. They simply represent "reality" for the person.

Addicts and criminals, however, tend to think mostly or all the time in distorted ways. These distortions help them to justify and rationalize criminal and addictive behavior, and not take responsibility for their actions.

Researchers have identified many thinking distortions that people use. Research also shows that people have personal styles of thinking based on which thinking distortions they find comfortable. Criminal and addictive thinkers consistently overuse certain basic thinking distortions.

With practice, you can learn to recognize which distortions you use and replace them with more accurate and effective ways of thinking.

Some of the thinking distortions overlap, and some are harder to understand than others. Don't worry too much about getting them all right the first time—you'll have lots of chances to identify the different thinking distortions in your own thinking. Here are some of the major thinking distortions that criminals and addicts use:

- extreme thinking (all-or-nothing thinking)
- overgeneralization
- personalization
- magnification and minimization
- jumping to conclusions
- selective focus
- concrete thinking
- actor vs. observer bias
- closed thinking
- emotional reasoning

Extreme Thinking (All-or-Nothing Thinking)

Extreme thinking is also called ***all-or-nothing thinking.*** Everything is viewed as either one extreme or the other. Extreme thinking says there is no middle ground. The world is either black or white. There are no shades of gray. Extreme thinking *divides*. Here are some examples:

- "Everybody always . . . "
- "Nobody ever…"
- "Everything I do goes to hell."
- "Nothing ever works out."

Or it can go to the other extreme:

- "I can do no wrong."
- "I always make good choices."
- "My way is always the right way."

Facilitator Note

Aaron Beck, a pioneer of cognitive-behavioral therapy, refers to this as "primal" thinking in that it is absolute, ego-centric, and occurs in the earliest stages of information processing.

Facilitator Note

It is very helpful to keep this list of thinking distortions in plain view of all participants during class. This can also be done with the key definitions. You may choose to write these thinking distortions on a flip chart or on posters that can be used during each session. Creating these posters or flip charts could be an art project for the participants.

Extreme thinking says there is no middle ground. The world is either black or white.

Extreme thinkers say it's okay to use alcohol or other drugs because "*All* my friends use" and "Since *every*body knows that *every*body steals, why shouldn't I?"

For an extreme thinker, the world looks like figure 9.

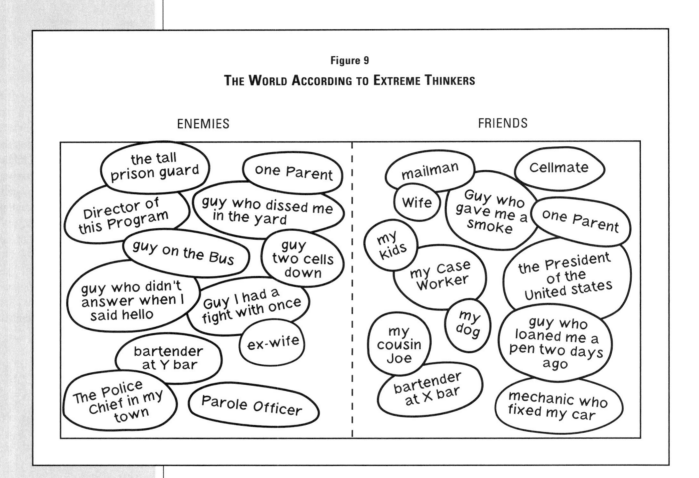

Figure 9
THE WORLD ACCORDING TO EXTREME THINKERS

ENEMIES | FRIENDS

Extreme thinking *distorts* the way you see the world. In figure 9, all people are either enemies or friends. Extreme thinkers place everyone they meet into one of the two boxes. The result: Once someone is placed in the "enemies" box, it's very hard to move that person to the "friends" box. On the other hand, it's easy to move someone from the "friends" box to the "enemies" box. Over time, the "enemies" box starts to get really crowded, and the "friends" box empties out (see figure 10).

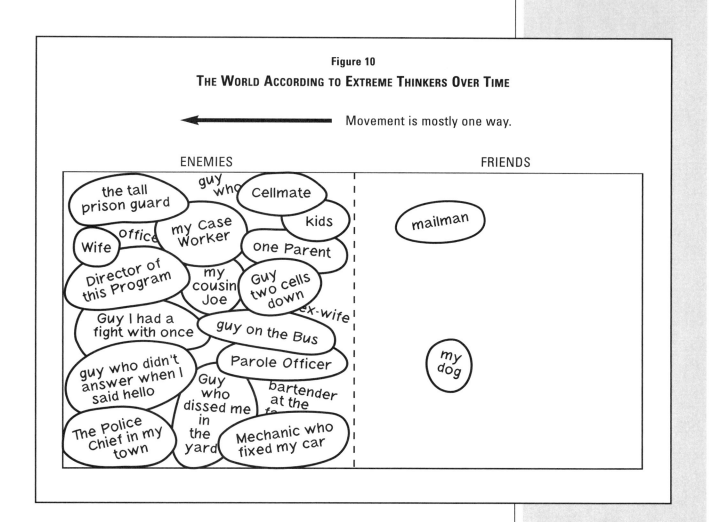

Figure 10

THE WORLD ACCORDING TO EXTREME THINKERS OVER TIME

← Movement is mostly one way.

ENEMIES   FRIENDS

the tall prison guard • guy who • Cellmate • kids • Office • my Case Worker • Wife • one Parent • Director of this Program • my cousin Joe • Guy two cells down • Guy I had a fight with once • guy on the Bus • ex-wife • guy who didn't answer when I said hello • Parole Officer • Guy who dissed me in the yard • bartender at the • The Police Chief in my town • Mechanic who fixed my car

mailman

my dog

In truth, very few people are truly enemies or truly friends. Most people you come in contact with fit into neither category. Instead, they are in a large, neutral middle category of neither friend nor enemy.

Facilitator Note

It is important to point out that movement between boxes (from enemy to friend or vice versa) is determined by how the participant thinks, not by the behavior of the other. Even if a behavior by the other would seem to merit that a shift be made, the thought reaction to that behavior determines whether the shift will take place.

Unfortunately, extreme thinking about the world, ourselves, and others (good/bad, safe/not safe, enemy/friend, trust/don't trust) leads us to extreme feelings and behaviors. We trust people until the first time they let us down, and then we hate them. We are successes or failures, heroes or zeroes. The world is either fair or not fair. We get angry, even abusive with people, or maybe feel hopelessly depressed about things. The result is a mental map that is so distorted, so limiting, that it operates almost like a personal mental prison, confining you to a very restricted vision of life.

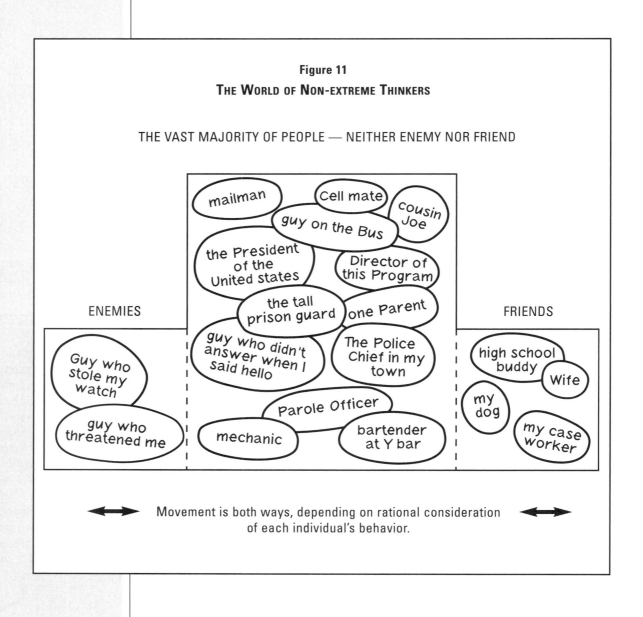

Figure 11
THE WORLD OF NON-EXTREME THINKERS

THE VAST MAJORITY OF PEOPLE — NEITHER ENEMY NOR FRIEND

mailman

Cell mate

cousin Joe

guy on the Bus

the President of the United states

Director of this Program

the tall prison guard

one Parent

ENEMIES

guy who didn't answer when I said hello

The Police Chief in my town

FRIENDS

Guy who stole my watch

high school buddy

Wife

Parole Officer

my dog

guy who threatened me

mechanic

bartender at Y bar

my case worker

Movement is both ways, depending on rational consideration of each individual's behavior.

Examples of Extreme (All-or-Nothing) Thinking

➤ List three examples of extreme thinking that relate to being chemically dependent, about other people, and about criminal behavior.

EXAMPLE: "Unless you are homeless, half-deranged, and sleeping in the gutter, you're not really an addict or alcoholic." (about alcohol or other drugs)

EXAMPLE: "You either respect me or you don't." (about others)

EXAMPLE: "Everybody steals; I just got caught." (about criminal behavior)

1. _____

_____

2. _____

_____

3. _____

_____

Unfortunately, extreme thinking about the world, ourselves, and others leads us to extreme feelings and behaviors.

Facilitator Note

Each of the sections on individual thinking distortions asks the participant to come up with examples of that distortion. It is very valuable for you to take the time to come up with your own list beforehand. This will help you to quickly determine whether or not the examples provided by the participants fit with the particular distortion under discussion.

Facilitator Note

Whenever examples are provided in the workbook and additional examples are sought from the participant, you will want to make sure that participants don't simply copy the example provided.

Overgeneralization

Overgeneralization is a thinking distortion that says because something happened once or twice, it must always be true. Overgeneralization is the basis for a lot of our problems, including *prejudices* of every kind.

Overgeneralizing thinkers tend to believe that if one person lies to them, then "You can't trust nobody." They may decide that because something happened once, it will always happen again under the same circumstances. It sounds silly until you think about how people overgeneralize about a person's skin color, religion, or gender.

Prejudice

Prejudice is a negative judgment or opinion of something or someone that is already decided beforehand and is not based on evidence.

Think of all the generalizations about people *you* have made over the years. "All [those people] are _____." You can fill in the blank as to who "those people" are and what "those people" are like. It doesn't matter what you put in the blanks. To say all people in a group are always one way or another is distorted thinking.

Overgeneralizing thinkers take a single or isolated event and turn it into a law of the universe: "That's just the way things are," they tell themselves. "Everybody lies." "Everybody steals." "All [those people] are [like that]—I know because I've met some of them."

**Overgeneralizing thinkers
rarely question these distortions.
In their minds, it's just "reality."**

Examples of Overgeneralization

➤ List some examples of overgeneralization that you have thought, said, or heard about other people, about the world, about chemical use, and about criminal behavior.

EXAMPLE: "Everybody is out for themselves." (about others)

EXAMPLE: "The world should be fair." (about the world)

EXAMPLE: "Everybody I know uses." (about alcohol or other drug use)

EXAMPLE: "Everybody steals." (about criminal behavior)

1.   _____

   _____

2.   _____

   _____

3.   _____

   _____

4.   _____

   _____

Facilitator Note
Make sure participants don't simply write the examples listed as their answers. Encourage them to think of situations where they've overgeneralized. These might include some of their stereotypes of the opposite gender.

Personalization

Personalization is a thinking distortion that says everything that happens around you is always all about you. Personalization makes all events somehow related to your life, even when there is no real connection. You think other people's actions and reactions are directed specifically at you every time. Even if others *don't* do something, you think that says something about you, too. Either way, it's all about *you*.

You may think an officer disrespects you if he doesn't respond to your request immediately. You believe it must be because he dislikes you. It doesn't occur to you that maybe it has nothing to do with you at all. You think rules are changed just "to get you to go off" or that your family doesn't answer the phone because they don't care about you (otherwise they'd sit around all day waiting for you to call, right?). You think the parole officer just had it out for you, and that's why he made you take all those urine analyses.

EXERCISE **12** EXERCISE

Examples of Personalization

➤ Give three examples of recent events that you personalized—events you thought were all about you but probably weren't. What went through your mind at the time of each event?

1. _____

_____

_____

_____

2. _____

_____

_____

_____

3. _____

_____

_____

_____

Sometimes you can magnify or minimize the importance of some event to the point of distorting it.

Magnification and Minimization

Sometimes you can magnify or minimize the importance of some event to the point of distorting it. Either you take the event out of context and blow it out of proportion or you play down the event's impact or significance. This is usually done to explain or justify your actions (or inactions) and to excuse the results of your behavior. Magnifying or minimizing tells only *part* of the truth. ***Magnification*** and ***minimization*** are distorted ways of thinking about the world, yourself, and others.

Here are some examples of magnification:

- "I'm late for work, so screw it, I'm not going."

- Automatically believing that something negative said to you is a personal attack.

- "I've been through a lot, so who can blame me for what I did?"

Here are some examples of minimization:

- "It wasn't that bad."

- "My using only hurts me."

- "It only happened once."

- "I caught a case."

- "Anybody can get a DUI."

When you blow things out of proportion, a minor confrontation becomes a major threat. When you make something seem worse than it really is, you respond strongly to everything related to it. When you minimize, you may try to dismiss the results of serious behavior, to convince yourself and others that it's no big deal.

EXERCISE **13** EXERCISE

Examples of Magnification and Minimization

➤ Give three examples of areas in your life that you tend to magnify (blow out of proportion).

1. _____

_____

2. _____

_____

3. _____

_____

➤ Give three examples of areas in your life that you tend to minimize (dismiss as less important than they are).

1. _____

_____

2. _____

_____

3. _____

_____

Jumping to Conclusions

When you are ***jumping to conclusions,*** you think you know where things are headed and make a snap decision with little or no evidence. You behave as if you are

- a mind reader—you instantly assume you know the reasons someone is reacting toward you in a certain way, or

- a fortune-teller—you predict or anticipate how things will turn out without waiting for the evidence.

Either way, you don't wait around for the facts, because you have already reached your conclusion.

An extreme form of this distortion is called the "self-fulfilling prophecy." You go into a situation looking for something to happen. You are then on the alert. If it happens, you are self-righteous about it: "I *knew* it." The problem is, your idea of how it was going to play out actually *determines* the outcome for you.

For example, what if you came into treatment expecting that the staff would just try to "tear you down," guessing they are out to terminate you as quickly as possible, just like they did in the last two programs you were in? You would jump to the conclusion that anything the staff did was an attempt to make you fail. You wouldn't bother doing any of the work. You'd think, "Why should I? I'm just going to get kicked out anyway." So after a few days or weeks of overreacting and not doing any of the work, you really *are* kicked out of the program. You walk out the door saying, "I told you so." But did you *know* what was going to happen, or did you *create* what happened?

EXERCISE **14** EXERCISE

Examples of Jumping to Conclusions

➤ Briefly describe two times when you jumped to conclusions and were wrong.

1. _____

_____

2. _____

_____

➤ What did you think when you found out the truth?

1. _____

2. _____

Selective Focus

Selective focus is a thinking distortion that means you pick and choose certain parts of an event or situation and focus only on those. What you focus on may be something good or bad. If some facts don't support what you already believe, you block them out. As a criminal and addictive thinker, you are probably an expert at this. You try to control the focus so you can justify your behavior.

For example, depressed people focus only on the negative. They don't ignore the good; they simply don't hear or see it. When you are looking at the criminal complaint against you, for example, you focus on the one or two small errors in the report, rather than the majority of the complaint that is true. Or during a disagreement with staff, you focus only on the one thing they said that you did not like.

EXERCISE **15** EXERCISE

Examples of Selective Focus

In a group discussion, an inmate was receiving feedback from his peers on his progress in treatment. Several members of the group told him they thought he was doing better. They said he was making progress completing his assignments, doing his unit job, and paying closer attention in group. But he still wasn't willing, they said, to talk about his crime or his addiction in group.

Later, a peer asked him how things went in group. The inmate said, "They all kept attacking me for not telling them about my crime."

Facilitator Note

When this situation occurred another time, the participant's response was just the opposite. He heard none of the criticism and reported, "They all told me I was doing well."

Either way, optimist or pessimist, low self-esteem or grandiose view of self, this thinking distortion is selective focus.

➤ How is the story on page 79 an example of selective focus?

_____

_____

_____

➤ Give an example of when you did something like that.

_____

_____

_____

Concrete Thinking

With ***concrete thinking,*** you focus on the specifics of an event or situation, but you don't get the message behind the situation. You take things literally, at face value, and have trouble ***generalizing*** from one event to the next. Because you treat each learning event as unique and disconnected, you fail to learn the general rules behind them. That's why you have trouble learning from your mistakes.

Concrete thinking is almost the opposite of overgeneralization—it's *under*generalization. For example, if you get a ticket for running a stop sign, you decide not to run that particular stop sign again. But you continue to run *other* stop signs. If you are told to stop using drugs, you use only alcohol because, in your mind, alcohol is not a drug.

Generalizing

Generalizing is the mental process of figuring out the common aspects of different events or things and then being able to draw accurate conclusions from them.

Because you can't generalize from one situation to another, you don't learn from past experiences. You also don't think far enough ahead to see the outcome of your behavior. That's why you repeat the same self-defeating behavior.

One definition of <u>insanity</u> is doing the same thing over and over and expecting different results.

EXERCISE 16 EXERCISE

Examples of Concrete Thinking

➤ Give an example of something in your life that fits the definition of *insanity* given above, or when you failed to think things through and ended up doing something really stupid. (By the way, being able to admit this is the first step to changing.)

_____

_____

_____

Facilitator Note
Many therapists believe that concrete thinking is the thinking distortion that trips up criminal thinkers the most. They often have a very difficult time abstracting lessons derived from their experience. It may require considerable feedback over time from staff and group members to help some offenders begin to remediate their problems with concrete thinking.

Actor vs. Observer Bias

Actor vs. observer bias is a tough thinking distortion to understand, but it's one that all people can relate to.

As humans, we tend to justify our negative behavior and blame other people or events when things go wrong. We often overlook how our attitudes and actions contributed to the situation. This distortion means that when you are an *actor* in a situation, you tend to focus only on the situation outside of you.

Don't forget that you have at least some control over the situations you "find" yourself in.

You forget that you

- pick and choose the situations you are in, at least in part,

- are a *part* of situations you are in, and

- have choices about how you deal with each situation.

When you simply *observe* a situation that you are not a part of, you are able to look at both the actor(s) *and* the situation. Ever see two guys get into a fight and then listen to their stories later? Each one blames the other for being a jerk. Neither one sees the part he played in the conflict.

If *you* were in the fight, you may justify your behavior by saying things like, "He was asking for it," "I had to protect myself," or "I found myself in a situation . . ." as if you weren't there and had nothing to do with your own behavior! You forget that you have at least *some* control over the situations you "find" yourself in.

Most of the time you have a lot of control.

Another example of actor vs. observer bias is when you are arrested, you say you "caught a case," like it was some kind of cold. "I caught a case" makes it seem as if you didn't have anything to do with the fact that you decided to go into the convenience store with a gun to rob it, and it didn't go down as planned. This distortion makes you think *you* were the victim; you just "found" yourself in a bad situation.

This thinking distortion leads you to think that you have little or no control over the situations you are in, and so you have few choices. Because you think others are responsible for the situation, you see yourself as the blameless victim. If you're the victim, any negative consequences or outcomes aren't on you.

Examples of Actor vs. Observer Bias

➤ Give a recent example of when the words "I found myself [doing something]" came out of your mouth.

_____

_____

_____

➤ What control did you have in picking the situation? If you think it was completely unavoidable, explain why.

_____

_____

_____

➤ What control did you have in what happened?

_____

_____

_____

Closed Thinking

Closed thinking means not listening to or trusting new information. When your thinking is closed, no one can convince you of anything more than you already "know." You lack self-awareness and aren't open to any new way of looking at things or doing things.

You argue that you're not open to new thinking or new behavior because it's brainwashing and "that's not the real you." You think you have to be true to yourself, right? Who cares if it means life behind bars on the installment plan, hepatitis, or even AIDS? You gotta be you. You don't listen to new ideas because no one has anything to tell you anyway.

What you call "brainwashing" the rest of the world calls education and personal growth. What you call "being true to yourself" the rest of the world calls willful ignorance.

EXERCISE **18** EXERCISE

Example of Closed Thinking

➤ Describe a time when you were absolutely closed-minded about something, when you weren't going to listen to anything anybody had to say and were going to do things your own way.

_____

_____

_____

_____

Emotional Reasoning

In *emotional reasoning,* feelings are facts. Your feelings are the ultimate guide to how you think about things and what you do. You react according to what you *feel,* basing your actions on emotions instead of on what you *think.* In fact, you may not even be able to see the difference between the two.

What gets lost with emotional reasoning are the thoughts that created the feelings in the first place. You have buried those thoughts and come to believe that your emotions just reflect the way things are. If it feels bad, then you shouldn't have to do it. If it makes you feel good or "right," then you're entitled to do it. When you *feel* like doing something, then you *will* do it. If you don't feel comfortable with something, then you think you shouldn't have to do it.

For example, you may complain that part of treatment is boring, so you decide you shouldn't have to put up with it. Or you say, "There's too much pressure in here. I can't change all at once" so you quit.

You also say "I feel" when you are really talking about what you're thinking: "I *feel* like I'm being treated unfairly" rather than "I *think* I am being treated unfairly." That type of emotional reasoning is an attempt to put the problem on others who have "created" these emotions in you—and it takes you off the hook for what you think.

■

In emotional reasoning, feelings are facts.
Your feelings are the ultimate guide to
how you think about things and what you do.

Facilitator Note
Remember: Feelings almost always arise as the result of thoughts. It is not the other way around, even though feelings may play an important role in the development of thinking patterns, by reinforcing the thinking that created them.

Examples of Emotional Reasoning

➤ Give two examples of making decisions based upon your emotions or feelings instead of taking time to think things through more carefully.

1. _____

   _____

2. _____

   _____

One More Look at Thinking Distortions

As humans, we all use some of these thinking distortions to a degree. As a criminal and addictive thinker, however, you tend to use them to an extreme, even when doing so leads to serious consequences. You don't fully think things through or think far enough ahead.

You probably noticed that some of these thinking distortions are similar and overlap each other. You can use several at the same time. While thinking distortions may help you deal with your criminal and addict "accountability problem" by helping you justify your behavior, they really lead you to trouble. (Remember: Distorted thinking leads to distorted thoughts, which lead to extreme behavior.) By not taking responsibility for your behavior, you don't have to change—you just hope you'll get lucky or that bad situations won't "find" you again. By learning to identify and

Facilitator Note

Point out that all people use thinking distortions to some extent. Simply using them doesn't make you a criminal or addict. The point is that both criminals and addicts use them frequently and take them to extremes. Stress the importance of learning new ways of thinking.

challenge these distortions, you begin to take responsibility for your behavior and to change your way of thinking. While you probably can't ever remove these distortions completely, you can, over time, develop tools to deal with them.

Consider how these thinking distortions have created problems in your life—for yourself and for others. Your distorted views of yourself, others, and the world have negatively affected your relationships with others, contributed to your alcohol and drug use, and led to your incarceration.

Now you are ready to start identifying the thinking distortions you use and adding them to your Thinking Reports. You can also begin imagining new, alternative behaviors—different ways of responding to the situation— that would be more effective and could help keep you out of trouble. Complete the "thinking distortions" part of the Thinking Report on page 63 of part 2.

Facilitator Note

Now the participants are ready to complete another area of the Thinking Report in exercise 9b on page 63. Help them identify additional alternate behaviors and thinking distortions for their Thinking Report.

The major thinking distortions of criminals and addicts are listed on page 67.

Criminal and Addictive Thinking Patterns

Facilitator Note

The following pages on criminal and addictive thinking may be best presented in lecture format rather than as a reading assignment, particularly if your group participants have a low reading level or learning disabilities. This may also be true of the introductory material for each of the individual thinking patterns. Presenting the ideas first in lecture format and then as a reading assignment is optimal.

Facilitator Note

When an offender says, "I feel [this]," he usually means "I think [this]." It is important to interrupt and help him rephrase his statement by replacing "I feel" with "I think." Example: "I feel I was taken advantage of" really means "I think I was taken advantage of." Thoughts precede feelings and behaviors, and it is important that the program participant understand which is which.

Thinking distortions are about *how* you think; criminal and addictive thinking patterns are more about *what* you think. Thinking patterns are habits of thought—types of thoughts a person uses so often that they just seem to come naturally. The thinking distortions you use—*how* you think—have a lot to do with the patterns of thoughts that you develop—*what* you think.

As a criminal and an addict, you have developed both criminal and addictive thinking patterns. These thinking patterns aren't all the thoughts you have, but they do dominate your thinking. This leads to trouble.

The good news is, you can change your patterns of thinking with a little help and a lot of effort.

This workbook and your therapists will provide the help; *you* have to supply the effort. No one can do it for you.

We have identified nine criminal thinking patterns and nine addictive thinking patterns. You will notice that some criminal and addictive thinking patterns are very similar or even the same. That's because criminality and addiction are both, to a large degree, *thinking* problems before they become *behavior* problems.

The criminal and addictive thinking patterns are listed on the table on the next page.

As you can see, the two groups of thinking patterns are very similar. Because of this, you can work on them together. Your efforts to change one will reinforce your work on the other. The only catch is, you have to accept that you must recover from both criminality *and* addiction— you can't pick one and leave the other.

Criminal Thinking Patterns	Addictive Thinking Patterns
• victim stance	• self-pity stance
• "good person" stance	• "good person" stance
• "unique person" stance	• "unique person" stance
• fear of exposure	• fear of exposure
• lack-of-time perspective	• lack-of-time perspective
• selective effort	• selective effort
• use of power to control	• use of deceit to control
• seek excitement first	• seek pleasure first
• ownership stance	• ownership stance

Criminal Thinking Patterns

Studies have shown that the decision to commit most criminal offenses occurs within ten minutes of the crime itself. That is, while criminals may think about committing crime for a long time without acting, they decide to act on the spur of the moment. Criminal thinking patterns are what allow the criminal to indulge in thoughts of crime and then suddenly act on those thoughts. Criminal thinking patterns are not exclusive to criminals.

Noncriminals may also have thoughts from time to time that fit in one or more of the categories of criminal thinking patterns. The difference is they don't act on them. Criminals, on the other hand, tend to have thoughts consistent with many or even all of the categories. Criminals use criminal thinking patterns more frequently and across the entire range of their life situations. And criminals act on those thoughts.

Criminal Thinking Patterns

Criminal thinking patterns are the types of thoughts that say it is okay to violate others or the property of others.

It's not your last crime that got you here; it's your first.

Thoughts that suggest, justify, or promote committing acts that violate others or the property of others most likely fit into one or more of the criminal thinking patterns categories.

You will notice that some of the criminal thinking patterns listed on page 89 are called "stances." A stance is a position you take to show yourself to the world. It is like an image or a pose. These poses are for the benefit of others, to make others see you as you want to be seen. Taking a stance is also a way for you to create a self-identity, to give you a sense of yourself. Without a true sense of reality and identity, all people tend to feel empty and worthless. Stances do not come from inside you. They are like masks or costumes. They are essentially fake. As a criminal thinker, you adopt a stance out of defensiveness or desperation. You fear that without your stances, you're really a nothing. You "put on" the front or mask and assume the role of victim, good person, unique person, or owner of whatever you want. Or you may truly believe that you and you alone are unique and powerful, entitled to get whatever you want.

You began adopting these stances at a very young age, and it didn't take long before you forgot that it was just a role you were playing. You came to believe, mistakenly, that your stances are who you really are. That's why all criminal thinkers cling to their thinking patterns so desperately, even though those patterns are making their lives miserable.

The remaining criminal thinking patterns identify unhealthy ways of thinking that you return to over and over when faced with life's challenges. Again, you probably began using them as a child and came to rely on them more and more as you got older.

You will learn to recognize these patterns in your thinking and begin to see their connection to the tired, old, dead-end journey of your criminal life. You will realize that there is a way out after all. You will recognize and challenge your criminal thinking patterns. You will give up your pretend life, the self-defeating role of a criminal.

Victim Stance

The first criminal thinking pattern is *victim stance.* In victim-stance thinking, you view yourself as a victim first. It doesn't matter what you have done to victimize others. The victim stance is a common way to defend yourself when you are held accountable for your behavior. The victim stance allows you to blame others for the situations you usually have created for yourself. You make many excuses and point the finger at others, claiming you were the one who was really wronged. And because you think you were wronged, you think your behavior is justified.

VICTIM-STANCE TYPES

A "stance" is a pose or posture or image the criminal thinker adopts. There are many types of victim-stance thoughts the criminal thinker will use to create an "I-am-the-victim" position. Here are some examples:

The victim of family:
> The criminal thinker blames the disadvantages of his home life—how he was mistreated, abandoned, or poorly nurtured by his family. (Of course, others in the same family may not have made criminal choices.)

The victim of society:
> The criminal thinker points to poverty, race, or neighborhood disadvantages, or blames unfair pressure or influence by peer groups. He will also claim the courts, law enforcement, schools, POs, correctional facilities, and other institutions have failed him or are out to get him.

The ex-con victim:
> The criminal thinker offers his criminal record as the reason why he can't possibly succeed in the world using noncriminal behaviors. He argues that society's mistrust of convicted criminals leaves him no options.

The victim of heredity (birth):
> The criminal thinker will claim he is simply "no good," "an outcast of the universe," or "born to lose."

Victim-stance thinking helps you gain the sympathy of the person who is confronting you or puts the focus onto that person or someone else—anything to take the heat off yourself.

Again, victim-stance thinking is used to justify your behavior to yourself and to others who hold you accountable. You blame just about anyone or anything for your crime except yourself—even though *you're the one who committed the crime.* "Someone else" was stupid. "Someone else" snitched you out. "Bad luck" got you arrested. "Fate" was against you. "Society" set you up to fail. All of it is just a way of saying, "It's not my fault."

 EXERCISE 20 EXERCISE

Blaming Others

As a criminal thinker, you blame others to get sympathy and to take the focus off yourself. Examples of blaming are

- "I wouldn't be this way if my father didn't drink."
- "The trouble with you is, you're always looking at me in a critical way."
- "I couldn't do it because he got in my way."

➤ Give two examples of how you've blamed other people or situations for your problems. Why did you think the other person or situation was at fault and you were not the one responsible?

1. _____

_____

_____

Facilitator Note

Offenders typically struggle to connect consequences with actions. (For more on the confusion between cause and effect, see the "Lack of Time Perspective" section beginning on page 126.) This may be a good place to introduce the idea that all actions and stances are the result of individual choice: It is the offender's choices—not happenstance, random events, conspiracy of others, or fate—that led him to where he is. Which thoughts he entertains is a choice; which thoughts he acts on is a choice.

2. _____

_____

_____

 EXERCISE **21** EXERCISE

Excuse Making

As a criminal thinker, you make excuses for everything. Whenever you are held accountable for being irresponsible or for committing criminal acts, you make excuses to justify your behavior. Making excuses is just another way of trying to convince yourself and others that you're the victim, that it's not your fault. Here are some examples of common criminal thinking excuses:

- "I broke in because I needed the money. People should expect that when they pay us so little."

- "Everyone does it."

- "That purse was just sitting in the booth. I didn't steal it; I found it."

➤ Give three excuses you use for committing crimes.

1. _____

2. _____

3. _____

Correcting Victim-Stance Thinking

A **victim-stance** thinker needs to learn four new things to change:

Facilitator Note

You may choose to discuss the ways participants can correct their victim-stance thinking. This might best be done in a group setting. It is useful to challenge participants to uncover the rationalizations they use to keep themselves in the victim role. Ask them what the rewards are for them and whether it's worth it.

- Accept your role in creating the situation. You have to recognize the choices you made and the criminal and addictive thinking patterns you relied on that led you to your incarceration. You must begin to see how your choices and thinking patterns affected everything you did that was irresponsible, not just the crime you were convicted of.

- Become aware of others who grew up in similar conditions of disadvantage and unfairness yet did not develop criminal thinking patterns. They made choices to not violate others or the property of others. Life is not always fair. Some people have it tougher than others, but there is always someone who had it worse than you did who chose to live responsibly. *It's a choice.*

- Realize that you are incarcerated because you are, in fact, the *victimizer,* not the *victim.*

- Understand that thinking of yourself as a victim and presenting yourself to the world as a victim is a huge barrier to developing a responsible lifestyle. The only thing you (or anyone) can ever truly control is your own thinking and behavior. It is *your* responsibility to learn to do just that.

The only thing you (or anyone) can ever truly control is your own thinking and behavior.

Not Everyone Became a Criminal

➤ Think about friends and neighbors throughout your life
who had it tough but decided to lead a responsible life.
List three of them.

	First name	What was tough in this person's life?	What did this person decide to do with his or her life?
1.	_____	_____	_____
		_____	_____
2.	_____	_____	_____
		_____	_____
3.	_____	_____	_____
		_____	_____

➤ What have you learned from these examples that will
help you to change?

_____

_____

_____

Facilitator Note

See facilitator note on
page 96.

Facilitator Note

After completing exercise 22, ask participants the following question: "What rationalization have you used to keep yourself stuck while others moved on?" Participants may see that others with similar backgrounds did not make the same choices they did to engage in self-defeating criminal and addictive behaviors. So participants usually try to explain away these accomplishments. It is useful to challenge participants to uncover the rationalizations they use to dismiss the responsible success others have and continue with their irresponsible lifestyle.

"Good Person" Stance

The second criminal thinking pattern is the **"good person" stance.** When you adopt this thinking, you consider yourself to be a good person, no matter what. You work hard to present that image to others. In fact, you may not only consider yourself a good person, you may think you're better than others! You probably don't think you're a criminal thinker at all. But you are.

Here are several examples of "good person" stance thinking:

- "I'm a good person. Look, I help my grandmother with the groceries all the time."

- "There's nothing wrong with my behavior. All I did was sell a little dope, provide a service for my customers."

- "The neighbors treat me like a criminal when all I did was take their motorcycle for a little spin. They forget how nice I am to their kids."

As a criminal thinker, you use four main strategies to create and maintain the illusion that you are essentially a good person. These strategies are

- sentimentality
- selective memory
- excuses and rationalizations
- false comparisons and self-serving definitions

Sentimentality

Sentimentality involves viewing your motives for committing a crime as always "good" on some level. You can then think you are essentially a "good person," despite your crimes. This is a distorted view to justify a criminal action in your mind or to avoid feeling bad about what you've done. As a sentimental criminal thinker, you might

- Rob a bank and then give $20 to a homeless person on the street. You'll think you're a good person for the good deed you did.

- Carry around pictures of your kids while incarcerated, maybe even putting them on your journal or workbook cover, to show others what a loving dad you are.

- Make sure to tell everyone how you used some of your drug profits to help out family and friends.

This sentimental view of yourself tricks you into believing you're a good person, even though

- The $20 you gave the homeless person wasn't really yours to give away.

- You may have pictures of your kids because you love and care for them, but it's also possible that you display them to help you put on your "good person" stance.

- There are always strings attached when you help out family and friends. You expect the people you help to return the favor many times over down the road.

Your sentimentality is often contradicted by your criminal behavior. You may help an old lady across the street but rob an older couple later in the evening. Your good feelings one moment toward old people (or animals, kids, your mother, poor people, religion, and so on) are separated from other, criminal parts of your personality and life.

Selective Memory

As a criminal thinker, you tend to recall only the positive actions you've taken and not the negative ones. This "good person" stance strategy is called selective memory. While you may remember every drug-profit dollar you ever gave to friends and family, you conveniently forget about the guy who overdosed on the smack you sold. The "good person" stance thinker who is using selective memory will

Remember this	but will not disclose this
I gave my girlfriend money for a new coat three months ago.	➤ I steal from her purse whenever she's not looking.
My conviction is for robbery.	➤ I also committed domestic abuse but was never prosecuted.

Excuses and Rationalizations

Criminal thinkers often make excuses and try to minimize the harm they have done to others, which is another "good person" stance strategy. For example:

The excuse or rationalization	The bigger picture
Insurance will pay for it.	➤ The victim's insurance rates will go up, or the person's policy will be canceled, and everyone else's rates will rise, too. Plus, I violated the victim's sense of safety, which may take years to heal.
I only took money. I never killed anybody.	➤ The crimes I didn't commit don't magically make the crimes I did commit somehow okay.

False Comparisons and Self-Serving Definitions
As a "good person" stance criminal thinker, you will try to make yourself look good by continually pointing out that someone else is "worse" than you. The criminal hierarchy found in all correctional facilities is an example of the delusion that some crimes are somehow "better" than other crimes. It's another way of lying to yourself and others about the reality of your behavior.

The "good person" stance lie	The truth
I sell drugs as a service to others.	→ I sell drugs to get what I want at the expense of others.
I'm an entrepreneur, not a criminal.	→ Operating a criminal business makes me a criminal.
Murderers are better than rapists.	→ Both have committed a violation of the body and soul of another person.

Correcting "Good Person" Stance Thinking
To correct "good person" stance thinking, you need to learn three things:

- Your sentimental goodwill toward others is not consistent. If you want to truly become a good person, someone who helps others, you must do *no* harm to others at any time.

- Put yourself in the other person's shoes. Learn to look at things from the other person's point of view, particularly your victim's. Fully understand that you affect many people with your behavior.

- Your character is determined by the sum total of what you do and don't do, not just by isolated incidents. You are responsible for *everything* you do and don't do.

EXERCISE 23 EXERCISE

I Am Everything I Do

Your character is determined by *everything* you do and think. It is not based on an isolated event. The good you do does not erase the bad—both are true about you. To stop using the "good person" stance, you need to start seeing the whole picture of yourself.

➤ Make a "balance sheet" of your life. On one side, list the good things you have done. On the other, list the harm that you have done. Think about the whole picture of your life. Remember, you were not arrested for the good things you do.

The good I have done	The harm I have caused
1. _____	1. _____
_____	_____
2. _____	2. _____
_____	_____
3. _____	3. _____
_____	_____
4. _____	4. _____
_____	_____
5. _____	5. _____
_____	_____
6. _____	6. _____
_____	_____

If That Were Me, I Would . . .

One of the ways you use "good person" stance is to minimize or ignore the effect of your irresponsibility on others. For example:

- "So I didn't do anything for my mother on Mother's Day. So what?"

- "I don't know what the big deal is. They got their car back."

- "My girlfriend is so upset. She acts like she's the one that got arrested, not me. It's crazy."

- "So I didn't show up for work. That's not a crime."

Another way is to have unrealistic expectations of others:

- "Some friend. He thinks he's hot s--- now that he's manager and won't even let a buddy in, just because I don't have a shirt on."

- "My case manager didn't know the answer to that question. They're supposed to know everything, right?"

➤ If you could put yourself in other people's shoes and see the situation through their eyes, it would look a little different. Think of two people you've had a problem with recently. Write down how you'd feel and what you'd think if you were them.

Person #1

First name _____

What was the situation?_____

_____

_____

What would you have thought or felt in this person's shoes?

_____

_____

What effect did you have on him or her?

_____

_____

Person #2
_____

First name _____

What was the situation?_____

_____

_____

What would you have thought or felt in this person's shoes?

_____

_____

What effect did you have on him or her?

_____

_____

Sentimentality in Perspective

Sentimental criminal thinkers can easily list their good intentions or actions, but they rarely follow through with their caring behavior consistently over time. Usually good deeds are one-shot deals or only when they feel like it.

Sentimental thinkers may say:

- "I'm not really a destructive person. I'm really into beauty. You should see my artwork!"

- "I really didn't want to kick that dog, but he just kept barking. I really like animals."

- "How can you say I don't show concern for my mother just because I got into trouble? I take care of her when she's sick."

➤ List three people or things you claim to be sentimental toward, and then briefly describe how your behavior toward those people or things has been hurtful.

Person or thing you are sentimental about	How has your behavior harmed this person or thing?
1. _____	_____
	_____
	_____
	_____
	_____

Facilitator Note

The participants might believe they were "good" drug dealers because they never sold to pregnant women. You may point out that it's quite possible that they couldn't tell whether a woman was pregnant, especially if she was in her first trimester of pregnancy.

Person or thing you are sentimental about	How has your behavior harmed this person or thing?
2. _____	_____
	_____
	_____
	_____
3. _____	_____
	_____
	_____
	_____

"Unique Person" Stance

The third criminal thinking pattern is called the **"unique person" stance.** When you take a "unique person" stance, you are saying some or all of the following things:

- "I am a loner; I don't need anybody."

- "The [gang, city, 'hood] I came from is not like yours. I'm different—I'm a player."

- "I'm not willing to reveal too much about myself. I need to maintain my secrets."

- "The more I know that others don't, the better. I'm not about to share any kind of information."

- "I won't get caught because I'm too smart."

- "No one has ever gone through what I've gone through, so no one could ever understand me."

- "I'm [smarter, tougher, better, deserve more] than other people."

When you are in the "unique person" stance, you are vague, deceptive, and untruthful. You lie outright to confuse and mislead others. You withhold key information that could help solve a problem.

You will also be super-optimistic. Super-optimism is an unrealistic expectation that just because you think things should be a certain way, then that's the way they'll be. You commit crimes because you never think you'll get caught.

You believe that if you think it, then it must be that way.

Perfectionism is another characteristic of "unique person" stance thinking. This means you expect yourself to do everything perfectly right away, without practice or failure. You won't try things that don't come easily or that you fear you won't be the best at. Eventually, you stop trying to do anything worthwhile because doing so risks failure. That would mean you're not unique, special, number one.

All this is true *even though you have a long list of failures in your history.* Not only that, it is a big reason *why* you have so many failures. No one can succeed at anything worthwhile by trying it only once.

It's also probably true that you think you're special even in treatment. You think that your criminality is different or that because you're unique, your chemical use is an excuse—it means your behavior isn't truly criminal. And now that you've decided to change, you think, *Presto! You've changed.* Just like that. You think that you now understand everything and don't have to do any real change work.

Like the other criminal thinking patterns, "unique person" stance is just another way that you justify not being responsible or productive.

Correcting "Unique Person" Stance Thinking
In order to change your "unique person" stance thinking, you will need to

- learn to set realistic standards for yourself and others

- accept that you will make mistakes—it's inevitable for all human beings—and realize that you can learn from your failures

- understand that nothing of value ever comes easily

- begin to solve problems by finding out the facts first

- resist believing that you are different from others

- develop humility, an understanding of what you are and what you are not

That last one, develop humility, is one of the most difficult for criminal thinkers to understand because they confuse humility with humiliation. Yes, humility means not being arrogant or boastful, but it does *not* mean being weak or submissive. Humility is a position of strength, because it is grounded in honest self-knowledge and can therefore be trusted. When you claim to be a simple, decent person and then follow that up with responsible behavior, that's humility. No one can doubt you or bring you down because you are living your word, and you know the truth about yourself. And no one can take that away.

Humiliation, on the other hand, is the logical result of trying to live in a stance, or pose. Claiming to be a smart criminal and ending up behind bars is humiliation. When you set yourself apart from others in a "unique person" stance, you are inviting humiliation.

Humility means not being arrogant or boastful.

EXERCISE 26 EXERCISE

26a.
Uniqueness in Perspective:
"I'm Just an Ordinary Person"

➤ 1. This week when you are thinking about asking for something special because of your "uniqueness," stop and write down

What was the situation?

_____

_____

What did you do to stop yourself?

_____

_____

➤ 2. This week when you are thinking you are better than "ordinary" people, stop yourself and write down

What was the situation?

_____

_____

What did you do to stop yourself?

_____

_____

Facilitator Note

Because of their sense of entitlement and grandiosity, many participants will genuinely be baffled by this exercise. They will say, "I didn't ask for *anything* special." You or peers may have to help some participants with examples you have observed.

■ ■ ■

26b.
Uniqueness in Perspective:
"Thinking Won't Make It Happen"

When you act on super-optimistic thinking, disaster is sure to strike eventually. Here are some examples of super-optimistic thinking:

- "There's no way in the world I won't get that job."

- "Stop worrying about grocery money. As soon as this deal goes down, we'll be on easy street."

- "They've got nothing. I'm sure my case will be dismissed."

➤ Note two of your super-optimistic thoughts this week and write them down.

1. What was the thought?

_____

_____

Why doesn't that make sense?

_____

_____

What steps could you take for a positive outcome?

_____

_____

2. What was the thought?

_____

_____

Why doesn't that make sense?

_____

_____

What steps could you take for a positive outcome?

_____

_____

■ ■ ■

26c.
Uniqueness in Perspective:
"I'm Not Superman—and Neither Is
Anyone Else"

When you use "unique person" stance thinking, you expect perfection from yourself, giving yourself an excuse to give up or to not even try. Perfectionism also gives you an excuse for self-righteous anger toward people who don't act "perfectly." Examples of this type of thinking are

- "I didn't finish writing the paper because my typing wasn't good enough."

- "My day was ruined. I was only able to do three of the six things I'd planned."

- "I'm dropping my girlfriend. She's always acting so sweet, but yesterday I overheard her being rude to her friend."

➤ In the past week, how did you make a big deal out of something minor that someone else did?

_____

_____

➤ What were your thoughts at the time?

_____

_____

➤ What could you have said to yourself to stop?

_____

_____

➤ Recall when you quit something because it was hard and you couldn't do it perfectly. What was it?

_____

➤ What could you have said to yourself to keep going?

_____

Fear of Exposure

As a criminal thinker, you probably like to pose as fearless. In fact, your reckless behavior may give others that impression. You may even believe that you *are* invincible. The truth is, however, that you are consumed with fears: fear that you are a nobody, fear that others will find you out, fear of all your thoughts and actions being brought out into the open and judged. This is called **fear of exposure,** and much of your thinking is driven by it. One of your biggest fears is the fear of fear!

Like other criminal thinkers, you also expect injury or early death. There is a common belief among criminal thinkers that they will have a short life and painful death. You use this as an excuse to commit crimes.

You also are likely to fear any kind of putdown. You think that to tolerate a criticism would be to let someone else control you. You're so jumpy; you often view *positive* feedback as a putdown.

When you are challenged and feel put down, you sometimes experience the "zero state." In this state, you feel worthless, empty, like a nobody. You can't admit these feelings. To do so would mean losing control. So you hold the feelings inside, keep them hidden, sometimes even from yourself. This may result in physical problems that are usually associated with stress, such as knotted muscles and pinched nerves, stomach and intestinal discomfort, and frequent headaches.

This is all part of the criminal thinking pattern called fear of exposure. There are four main aspects of fear of exposure:

- fear of vulnerability
- lack of trust
- criminal pride
- zero state

Facilitator Note
A "live hard, die young, and leave a good-looking corpse" bravado pervades the criminal culture. This may be an example of fear of death sublimated and expressed as defiance of death.

Fear of Vulnerability

As a criminal thinker, you fear appearing weak and inadequate to anyone, even nonthreatening people such as young children. One reason is your fear of death or injury, a fear that you think about all the time.

You're also afraid that if you let anyone see the real you, you will be humiliated. Your fear of humiliation is powerful. It pushes you to commit a number of antisocial and self-defeating behaviors, such as

- getting into a lot of fights

- pushing away the people who genuinely care for you

There is a high price to pay for your fear of vulnerability. You have given up closeness with another person, *any* person. This is because you cannot be close to someone without being vulnerable to him or her. And that requires trust.

Lack of Trust

A major aspect of the criminal thinking pattern fear of exposure is a lack of trust. One reason for this is that when you are constantly trying to get away with criminal activity, you are *always* vulnerable to being exposed or caught. You've always got something to hide.

Your criminal behavior is your weak spot.

All someone has to do is call the cops and you're busted. Since you fear being exposed or caught and your criminal behavior makes you vulnerable, you're suspicious of everyone. You think just about everyone else is a con man, just like you. You don't even trust your criminal partners—and they don't trust you. Criminal thinkers are always holding back some information from their criminal associates. They are always trying to protect themselves by getting something on each other—*just in case.*

Criminal Pride

Criminal pride shows itself in fighting, bragging, refusing to admit you don't know something, and believing that your type of crime is better than the other guy's type of crime.

It is really important to you that you get what you think is "respect" from others. You are always thinking about who respects you and who doesn't. But think about it: If you had true *self*-respect, you wouldn't need the "respect" of others so badly.

The fact is, you don't have much true self-respect. Underneath it all, you're scared that without all your stances and postures, you are nothing.

Zero State

If you dare to think you are not unique or special, what little self-respect you have drops to zero. This is called the zero state. The zero state consists of these beliefs:

- You are nothing.

- Everyone else also believes you are worthless.

- Your "worthlessness" will last forever and can never be changed.

Criminal zero-state thinkers are also angry and want to victimize others. Being in the zero state is uncomfortable. You want to do something "powerful" to get yourself out of the zero state, like hurting other people.

In the zero state, your values are backward. You think normal, appropriate, and healthy behaviors are signs of weakness. This includes thinking and behavior such as

- the willingness to compromise with loved ones

- the ability to admit mistakes and take responsibility

- the willingness to learn from mistakes and move on

- the patience to set goals and work toward them, even at the risk of failure

Facilitator Note
The zero state typically occurs after exposure—after arrest or persistent challenge in group or any other revelation of their real motives, intent, thinking, and behavior.

The Continuum of Fear

What is healthy and unhealthy about fear can best be understood when it is seen on a continuum of fear—a range of how different people look at fear. The continuum of fear looks like this:

Figure 12
THE CONTINUUM OF FEAR

Too Afraid	Healthy Fear	No Fear
Has so many fears that he can't make a healthy decision	Has rational fears that guide him to take care of himself and motivate him to make healthy decisions for change	Fears nothing—thinks he's untouchable—and doesn't think he needs to make any changes

Both extremes are self-destructive. The law of all life is "Change or die." Living at either end of the continuum discourages and even prevents change. Most criminal thinkers shuttle back and forth between the extremes, spending very little time, if any, in the healthy middle.

Correcting Fear of Exposure

In order to change your fear of exposure, you will need to do the following:

- become more self-aware

- develop realistic expectations for yourself and others

- let go of false pride and accept a basic humility that helps you know who you really are—neither a "hero" nor a "zero"

- replace your desire for domination with a desire for cooperation and partnership—especially in your closest personal relationships

- learn to assess the integrity of others accurately

- come to trust honest and well-meaning people who can help you in life

- be guided by healthy and accurate fears rather than fear of the zero state or no fear

You have to work toward these goals steadily; try to learn a little something and practice it every day. Recovering alcoholics deal with the same things.

You may not like the idea of giving up your big-shot, hero status. But the truth is, it was a lie all along. If you were a hero, you wouldn't be where you are now: addicted to alcohol or other drugs and incarcerated. That may seem like the bad news, but it really isn't. When you give up the idea that you're some kind of superhero, you also get to give up feeling that you're worthless, empty, nothing. Because that's not true about you either. And *that's* the good news.

Now you just have to find what that "something" is. When you do, you will discover who you really are.

Inventory of Fears

➤ Complete the following sentence by placing an **X** next to each phrase that you can relate to.

When I think about changing my life, I fear that

____ Temptations will keep me from succeeding.

____ Change is too difficult.

____ My intentions are good, but I don't have the ability to change.

____ My family will reject me if I change.

____ My friends will reject me if I change.

____ I would have to be responsible and that's not possible for me.

____ I would make commitments I might not be able to keep.

____ I wouldn't like who I'd become.

____ I'd be too straight.

____ I'd be weak.

____ I'd lose my street smarts.

____ I wouldn't be able to relate to responsible people.

____ I'd be overwhelmed by it all.

____ I wouldn't be able to have any fun.

____ I'd be too vulnerable; opening up and being honest is too risky.

____ I'd be bored with responsible living.

Facilitator Note

The purpose of this exercise is for participants to face their fears regarding change. This would be an excellent exercise for a group discussion. Acknowledge that change is difficult, but essential in turning their lives around.

EXERCISE 28 EXERCISE

Learning to Bend

Because of their fear of exposure, criminal thinkers tend to be rigid in their thinking. The fact is, however, that a *real* man can bend and be flexible. Here are some examples of rigid fear-of-exposure thinking:

- "It's against my principles to give in."

- "What right did he have to question my motives?"

- "I'm not going to let him think I'm weak. No one puts me down."

➤ On which issues do you find it difficult to give in?

1. _____

2. _____

3. _____

Recall a time when you were overly sensitive to a challenge most people would consider normal.

EXAMPLE:

> *In group someone tells you, "I don't see you being willing to own up to your crime yet."*

➤ Describe the incident.

_____

_____

_____

➤ What was your first reaction?

_____

_____

➤ What could you tell yourself—how could you challenge your thoughts—so you could respond more flexibly?

_____

_____

➤ How could you have responded differently by being more flexible?

_____

_____

➤ List three things you can be truly proud of having done (that your conscience tells you are good and right).

1. _____

2. _____

3. _____

The Emotional Man

➤ This outline of a man represents your body. Take four colored markers, each representing a feeling or emotional quality you have, and draw where each of these feelings or emotional qualities exists in your body.

red = anger

green = envy

yellow = fear

blue = sadness

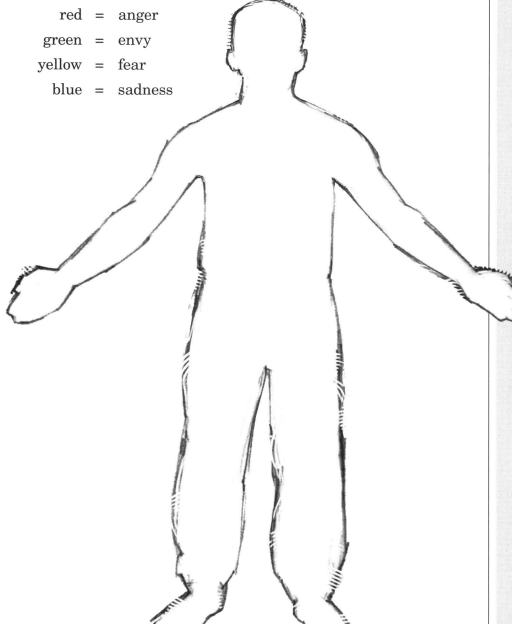

Facilitator Note

If the participants don't have colored markers available to them, have them identify their feelings and emotions on the outline using circles with the letter placed inside the circle.

A for **anger**

E for **envy**

F for **fear**

S for **sadness**

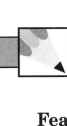

Fear as a Guide to Responsible Living

Fear is not necessarily a bad thing. Rational, healthy fears guide us every day. A rational fear of dying may keep you from jumping from a high place. A fear of crashing may lead you to drive sanely. A fear of losing everything you have may prevent you from taking a risky criminal venture or from gambling all that you own.

➤ What things do you do that you *should* be afraid of? List five of them, and then describe what could go wrong in each case. Assume the worst possible outcome.

You *should* be afraid of . . .   because it could lead to . . .

1. _____

   _____

2. _____

   _____

3. _____

   _____

4. _____

   _____

5. _____

   _____

Interrupting the Zero State

As you've learned, living in the zero state is unbearable and you will do almost anything to get out of it. Not realizing that the zero state is temporary, you fool yourself into thinking that anything—even incarceration—would be better. That's one way you justify your criminal behavior to yourself. Here are some examples of this kind of thinking:

- "I'd rather be serving time than be straight like you."

- "I can't stand it any more. I'm going to find some excitement."

- "There's no hope for me. I've been following the program and I have more problems than ever."

To interrupt zero-state thinking, you need to try to see the big picture of your life. One way is to identify the good things you have done or tried to do.

➤ List three things about you that are worthwhile:

- things you've done or tried to do that were positive contributions to others or to society

- qualities you have that, if used responsibly, could bring you success and help others

- something you've done in the past week that shows you are making progress in changing your criminal and addictive thinking

1. _____

_____

2. _____

_____

Facilitator Note

Here are two quick and simple optional exercises that can be done in a small group.

1. *The Musical Instrument Game:* Ask group members to take turns telling other participants what kind of musical instrument each of the others remind them of. For example, "You remind me of a [tuba, saxophone, bass drum, electric guitar, etc.] because of [these traits you have]." This is a relatively safe way for group members to expose each other and to reflect how they perceive one another. To avoid particularly nasty comparisons (participants will often try to find some way to put each other down), you may want to remind them that everyone will have a turn at this exercise. Honesty and respect should be encouraged.

2. *Something Positive:* Have each participant tape a paper on his back. The others take turns writing something positive on the paper about the person who is wearing it. The comments should be anonymous, so participants should write their comments in random order. When everyone is done, have the men remove the papers for each other, let them read the comments and then discuss the exercise.

3. _____

_____

■

At first, it is difficult to get out of the zero state by yourself. That is why one of the best ways to interrupt the zero state responsibly is to call someone you trust and talk it through.

EXERCISE **32** EXERCISE

Learning Trust

Facilitator Note

Trust is a big issue.

Participants need to learn to trust the right people and be willing to take risks. Point out that the participants are already working on this by sharing in group discussion.

As a criminal thinker, you have a problem with trust. For the most part, you don't trust others and they don't trust you. Or you trust the wrong people. Here are some examples of the trust problem in your thinking:

- "I don't see why my [parents, family, teachers] don't trust me. I've been straight for two weeks."

- "So I just met him on the street. He looks okay. Why shouldn't I trust him?"

- "I have a hunch he hasn't always been completely honest with me, so I'm not going to trust him."

- "All [teachers, therapists, doctors] are alike. You can't trust them."

➤ List some reasons why other people would trust you.

_____

_____

_____

➤ List some reasons why other people would *not* trust you.

_____

_____

_____

➤ Who do you trust?

1. _____

2. _____

3. _____

➤ Why do you trust them?

1. _____

2. _____

3. _____

➤ Are there people in your past who you *should* have trusted and listened to but didn't?

_____

_____

_____

➤ What do you need to change for others to trust you more?

1. _____

_____

2. _____

_____

3. _____

_____

As a criminal thinker,

you have a problem with trust.

Facilitator Note

Have participants answer the questions at the end of the case history on page 125 in a group discussion.

Case History

This is a true story that took place not long ago in a chemical dependency treatment program in a state correctional facility. It shows how fear of exposure and criminal pride manipulate and control the criminal thinker; it also shows how fragile and meaningless such false pride really is.

A therapist for a chemical dependency treatment program at a correctional facility brought in a box of roses in several different colors. He told the members of his group that day that they each had to wear a rose all day long. They could pick the color they wanted. The men were very resistant; they did not want to wear a rose. Since this was mandatory, however, they each reluctantly picked out the color they wanted and stuck the stem through a buttonhole or into a pocket. Nobody selected the pink roses.

As the men in the group went about their day, men in other groups started to notice the roses. First, they were teased about the roses. Then some of the other inmates asked if they, too, could have a rose. As they asked, they were invited to pick from the remaining roses. Soon all the roses were gone, including the pink ones.

As the day went on, more inmates asked to have a rose, and they were told there were none left. This made them mad and they made verbal protests. By the end of the day, kites (written inmate communication forms) were being submitted to the director of the program. They said that some men were receiving special treatment by being given roses to wear while others were being excluded. Some of the inmate kites were very angry and demanded fair treatment.

What happened in this story? Why did the men resist wearing the roses at first? Why were the pink roses left behind? What changed as the day went along? Why did it change? Why did men send angry written communications when they didn't get a rose? What does all of this say about the nature of criminal pride?

Instant Gratification

Instant gratification means satisfying a desire or need immediately, without planning or effort.

Impulsive

Impulsive means acting on the spur of the moment, without much thought or consideration. Most crimes are committed impulsively.

Lack-of-Time Perspective

Another feature of your thinking is a **lack-of-time perspective.** There are three parts to this criminal thinking pattern:

1. You do not learn from past experiences and do not think about the future. You see behaviors as isolated events. You do not clearly grasp the idea of *cause and effect,* which means that when you do A (cause), then B (effect) happens. Sometimes you even reverse the idea (thinking the result was really the cause). Therefore, you are likely to think, "This time will be different," and indulge the same thoughts and repeat the same behaviors that have failed you before.

2. You believe in the instant gratification of desires. Your philosophy is "I want it, and I want it *now*." You expect others to act on your demands immediately, and you tend to act impulsively in most areas of your life.

3. You expect to be a big success with only minimal effort and preparation, and you fantasize constantly about making the "big score." You do not set achievable goals or make realistic plans. You often base your decisions on whims and assumptions that are rarely supported by facts. You make choices based on what you *want* to be true rather than what is true.

As a result of these three problems, your thinking gets you into serious trouble regularly. You don't think things through. You don't consider the situation from several angles to see the possible consequences. Therefore, you lack the sound decision-making process you need for responsible living. Your decision-making is compromised in three ways:

1. You act impulsively, on the spur of the moment, to satisfy your need for instant gratification.

2. You avoid seeking facts, because it shows you don't know the answer and you may have to ask others for help.

3. You have tunnel vision. You focus only on what is in front of you and the easiest way to get it rather than seeing the whole range of options available.

The decisions you make tend to be the ones that inflate your image the most or else seem to be the easiest way. Sometimes, you make decisions by default. This happens when you avoid making a decision by refusing to recognize that a problem exists. When the consequences of failing to make a responsible decision hit you, as they always do, you claim to be a victim of random events you did not choose. You do not understand that refusing to choose is often a choice in itself.

Adding Up the Time

➤ Make a list of all the places you've been incarcerated. Include juvenile detention, jail time done even when you weren't prosecuted, detox, and every other place where you were detained by the justice system. Then list the amount of time you were detained. At the bottom, add up all the time you've done. If necessary, complete this exercise in a notebook.

Place of incarceration   Time done there

_____   _____

_____   _____

_____   _____

_____   _____

_____   _____

_____   _____

_____   _____

_____   _____

_____   _____

_____   _____

                              Total time _____

Facilitator Note

You may also want participants to add up the financial costs of their incarceration(s), such as money spent by the inmate, family, and friends on lawyer's fees, trips to visit the offender in correctional facilities, and phone calls from there; the financial costs to the victim and victim's family in property replacement and medical and mental health expenses (which may be particularly difficult for those who have not yet begun victim empathy work); the financial costs to the community in police, judges, court employees and courthouses, detox, corrections and treatment facilities and employees; and the financial costs of property destroyed or stolen. One way to accomplish this, in part, is to construct an estimated formula such as X amount of dollars per arrest, per month incarcerated, per day of trial, and for each court appearance.

Correcting the Lack-of-Time Perspective in Your Thinking

As exercise 33 shows, your desire for instant gratification, your inability to understand cause and effect, and your lack of planning have had a cost. They have cost you, your family, your victims and their families, and the rest of society. And they have cost *a lot*—in time, money, and meaningless suffering. To correct this disastrous thinking pattern, you need to do the following:

- change from thinking in terms of instant gratification to thinking in terms of goals

- identify your patterns of thinking and behavior that have had severe negative results in your life

- learn to base your current and future decisions on a thorough examination of the facts

- understand and accept that responsible payoffs are not immediate and that time, effort, and patience are needed to plan for and achieve worthwhile goals

 EXERCISE 34 EXERCISE

Responsible Choices

➤ Think about one of the crimes that you have been incarcerated for and list, as clearly as possible, five irresponsible choices you made that led to that crime. List them in the order that they occurred. In the second column, write down responsible alternative choices you *could* have made each time.

Crime: _____

_____

Irresponsible choices you made	Responsible choices you could have made
1. _____	_____
_____	_____
_____	_____
2. _____	_____
_____	_____
_____	_____
3. _____	_____
_____	_____
_____	_____
4. _____	_____
_____	_____
_____	_____
5. _____	_____
_____	_____
_____	_____

➤ What tends to happen when you make an irresponsible choice?

_____

_____

➤ What tends to happen when you make a responsible choice?

_____

_____

EXERCISE **35** EXERCISE

Sound Decision-Making Skills

Lack-of-time perspective in your thinking leads you to make many poor decisions that bring you trouble over and over again. This occurs mainly because of your unwillingness to get the facts you need to make a sound decision. Here are examples of this kind of thinking:

- "I wasn't going to look like an idiot by asking the driver, so I got on the wrong bus."

- "What is there to know about buying a car? You need one, you buy one."

- "No, I didn't call about the job. A friend told me they would never hire ex-cons."

Facilitator Note

If possible, exercise 35 should be completed as a group exercise. Because of a lack of healthy decision-making skills, the question "What are the most important facts you have to help you make this decision?" may be daunting. Due to their fear of exposure, participants will be inclined to leave the exercise blank—to not try at all. In group, this response may be mitigated somewhat if others also struggle with the question.

➤ What important decision are you currently faced with making (or will be in the near future)?

_____

_____

_____

➤ What are the most important facts you have to help you make this decision? The *facts* are the pieces of information about the decision that, taken together, point you in one direction or another.

_____

_____

_____

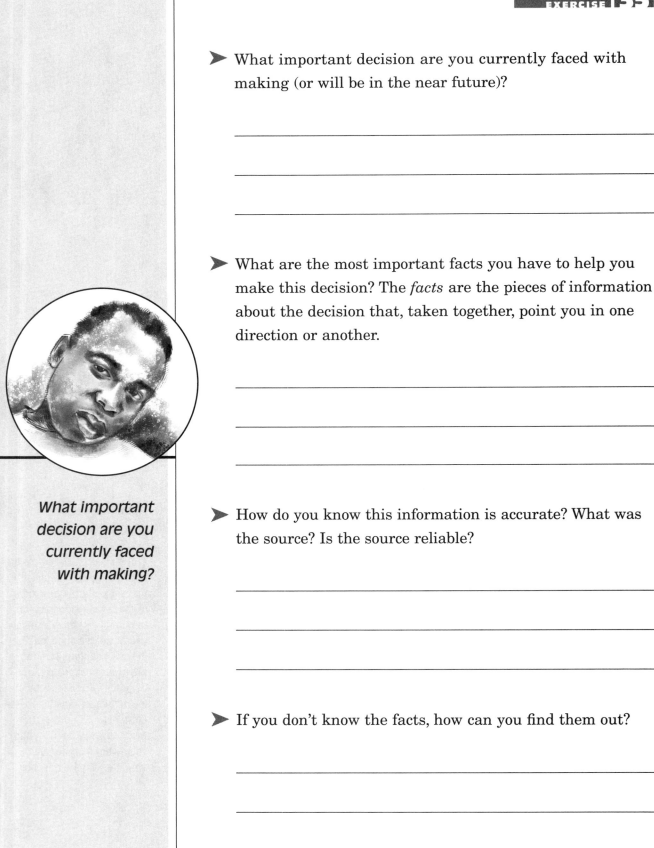

What important decision are you currently faced with making?

➤ How do you know this information is accurate? What was the source? Is the source reliable?

_____

_____

_____

➤ If you don't know the facts, how can you find them out?

_____

_____

_____

➤ When does the decision have to be made? How long do you have to make the decision?

_____

_____

_____

_____

➤ What are your alternatives? How do they stack up against each other?

_____

_____

_____

_____

➤ How do your alternatives fit with what you want in life, now and later?

_____

_____

_____

_____

Selective Effort

The sixth criminal thinking pattern you use is **selective effort.** People put forth *effort* not because it's necessarily fun, or provides a rush, or seems like the thing to do in the moment. Effort is not impulsive. It means putting a plan into motion. Work is effort. Study is effort. Training and exercise are effort. Doing what is required of you in this treatment program is effort.

As a criminal thinker, you use *selective* effort. In fact, you may do almost anything you can to avoid responsible effort. You may put out a great deal of energy, especially in your criminal pursuits. But when it comes to effort, you tend to avoid it at all costs. Usually you do this by saying, "I can't." What you really mean is, "I won't."

This is not to suggest that you don't start a lot of new projects. You've most likely had a lot of energy and were always busy cooking up one kind of a scheme or another. Sometimes you may even become totally preoccupied with one of your activities, to the point where you let go of nearly everything else, including eating and sleeping. But eventually you become bored with it, particularly if problems or setbacks result. Then it begins to seem more like effort, and that's when you quit.

You therefore tend to be selective about your efforts, like most criminal thinkers.

> **You either avoid something when you can't make a quick gain, or you bail out as soon as effort becomes necessary.**

When it comes to effort, you lose your energy really fast, despite your history of having a lot of energy for impulsive criminal activity.

Effort

Effort is a sincere attempt to exert yourself mentally or physically to achieve a goal.

Selective effort can be summed up in these mental traits:

- refuses to move through obstacles or stressful circumstances

- becomes bored with anything requiring work (effort) over time

- feels ***entitled*** to material things without having to earn them

EXERCISE 36 EXERCISE

Half-Finished Projects

➤ How many times have you started something positive only to get bored and quit midway through? Describe three projects you started but didn't finish. It could be a book you started reading but put down, going to school but dropping out, a woodworking or car repair project you left half-finished, and so on.

1. _____

2. _____

3. _____

➤ Now list some big projects or goals that you followed through to the end.

1. _____

2. _____

3. _____

Legitimate Job History

➤ Make a list of the legitimate (legal) jobs you've held in your life. List the job, how long you held the job, and why you left the job (you quit, were fired, or were laid off).

Job	Reason for leaving job	Time on job

Facilitator Note

Some participants may have never held a "real" job and may leave this exercise blank. Make sure they include only legitimate jobs, such as employment that required filing income taxes.

➤ What does this job history tell you about the effort you gave to responsible jobs?

_____

_____

Correcting Selective Effort

Correcting selective-effort thinking means giving up the "I can't (I won't)" attitude. No meaningful change is possible as long as you hold on to it. If you think about it, the "I can't (I won't)" attitude you made part of your personal thought map leaves you with only three options:

1. You can continue with your criminal behavior and spend your life in and out of correctional facilities or on the run.

2. You can commit suicide (and the suicide rate is very high among prisoners compared with the general population).

3. Or you can let go of the "I can't (I won't)" attitude and begin making the changes that will lead to recovery and a responsible life.

That's it. Three options.
We suggest option number three.

If you choose recovery and responsibility, you have changed "I can't (I won't)" to "I *must*." That may seem like a small thing, but it's not. Once you start saying, "I *must*," you have taken a huge step toward a different kind of life.

The second part of changing your selective-effort thinking is learning how to set goals and plan the steps to reach them. As a criminal thinker, you have a difficult time with this. Your track record for taking more than a few steps toward any meaningful goal is poor. This does not mean you can't learn how to succeed at setting goals and following through now. Using past failure not to try is just an excuse. You can learn to set a responsible goal and maintain responsible behavior as you move toward it simply by practicing taking one step today toward something better. You have heard that sobriety comes "one day at a time." The same is true of responsible living.

Today, practice taking one step toward something better.

Excuses

To be able to set goals and follow through on the steps to reach them, it helps to identify the excuses you use to not be responsible. One excuse is "I'm too tired." When faced with responsibility, you often claim you are too tired. Yet you have plenty of energy for irresponsible activities. In fact, your tiredness may really come from fear of failure, self-pity, and anger at being asked to delay your gratification. The truth is, whenever you can't pursue excitement or pleasure in the moment, you get angry. That's part of your criminal thinking pattern.

▶ What are some of the excuses you have made to try to get out of having to put forth responsible effort?

1. _____

   _____

2. _____

   _____

3. _____

   _____

4. _____

   _____

You Can—and You Must

You must adopt an attitude of *doing:* taking the first step toward something better, making an effort to try things differently, even if there doesn't seem to be an immediate payoff. Even if it doesn't look like fun. Even if there are obstacles. To do this, it's helpful to really understand what you can and can't do.

Some things you *can't* do	Some things you *can* do
You can't change anybody but yourself.	You *can* change yourself.
You can't change the past.	You *can* change the future.
You can't always get your own way.	You *can* change what you think and do when you don't get your own way.
You can't always get people to do what you want them to do.	You *can* change what you think and how you respond when people don't do what you want them to do.
You can't start your own company overnight.	You *can* get a job.
You can't always pick and choose the problems you have to face in your life.	You *can* decide how to handle these problems.
You can't change how people come at you.	You *can* change how you respond to them.

Here are some examples of "I can't (I won't)" selective-effort thinking:

- "Being a parent is boring—and raising the kids ain't my job anyway."

- "My wife asks too much of me. I care about her, but not enough to put up with her nagging."

- "If I can't be the boss, I don't want the job."

➤ What things do you usually say "I can't" to? Listen to yourself this week and write them down.

1. _____

2. _____

3. _____

One time this week, when you find yourself starting to say (or thinking about saying), "I can't," instead say, "I can" and go ahead and do it. Write down what happened.

➤ What was the situation?

_____

_____

➤ What were you thinking at the moment?

_____

_____

➤ What did you tell yourself to be able to say "I can"?

_____

_____

➤ How did people react when you actually did it?

_____

_____

➤ Write about a time in your life when you pushed yourself to your limits to reach a responsible goal.

_____

_____

_____

_____

_____

_____

_____

_____

_____

Setting Goals

➤ List three goals you would like to achieve in the future. *Keep them realistic and attainable.* (Playing in the NBA does not qualify. Becoming a doctor does not qualify. Getting a high school diploma or completing a job training course would qualify.)

Goal #1

_____

Goal #2

_____

Goal #3

_____

➤ List the steps you could take to reach each of these goals. List them in the order you think they should be done.

Steps to reach goal #1

1. _____

2. _____

3. _____

4. _____

5. _____

Steps to reach goal #2

1. _____

2. _____

3. _____

4. _____

5. _____

Steps to reach goal #3

1. _____

2. _____

3. _____

4. _____

5. _____

➤ List some barriers or obstacles, things that get in your way, that you may have to overcome to reach each goal.

Barriers or obstacles to achieving goal #1

1. _____

2. _____

3. _____

Barriers or obstacles to achieving goal #2

1. _____

2. _____

3. _____

Barriers or obstacles to achieving goal #3

1. _____

2. _____

3. _____

Facilitator Note

An excellent pamphlet that deals with these issues of power to control is *Power Plays* by Brenda Schaeffer (Hazelden, 1986). These issues are also dealt with in the *Socialization* module.

Use of Power to Control

As a criminal thinker, you often think in ways that involve the **use of power to control** others and get your own way. This power is not legitimate power, such as the power to create, to right a wrong, or to effect change for the better. It is not power earned through hard work, study, and the gaining of experience and knowledge. It is also not power that comes from discipline, self-control, and self-knowledge. Your criminal thinking type of power is none of these things. It is power used to manipulate, intimidate, humiliate, and dominate others for your own excitement and to get what you want.

The thinking that drives you to use power to control is motivated by selfishness. You do it because controlling others makes *you* feel good. It is a crude strategy to avoid the zero state (feeling like you are nothing) that we discussed earlier. Using power to control is also the direction your thoughts take when victim-stance thinking doesn't work for you. If you can't manipulate others by gaining their sympathy, you try to do it through fear and intimidation.

Examples of this kind of thinking include the following:

- "Do unto others before they do unto you."
- "Man, you don't know who you're messin' with."
- "I'm not letting no girlfriend tell me what to do."
- "The best defense is a good offense."
- "I can't stand getting bossed around at work."

Using power to control can involve in-your-face verbal or physical threats of force (actual threats or just suggestions of "bad things" that could happen). It can also be quiet, behind-the-scenes manipulation of others or slick con-man talk. No matter how it is used, chances are the thinking that leads you to use power to control has been with you a long time and dominates much of your life, through your

- **appearance**—dressing to look tough, pumping iron to appear bigger and more intimidating, wearing chains or tattoos, and so on
- **speech**—cold, threatening tone of voice and choice of words and phrases, such as "have I got a deal for you" cons and giving someone the silent treatment
- **facial expressions and body language**—using threatening looks, such as a stare-down, chest inflated and shoulders forward, jaw clenched, fists clenched, and other such gestures, postures, and expressions

As a criminal thinker, you often think in ways that involve the use of power to control others and get your own way.

- **sexuality**—seeing sex as a conquest, a hunt in which the partner isn't a human being you care for but something to outsmart or overpower and take advantage of

- **work and play**—seeing everything as a competition, me against you, only one of us can come out on top, a win-at-all-costs attitude that says, "I have to put you down, so you'll stay down"

- **parenting**—seeing your kids as your property who must obey your every command, rather than as your responsibility to be nurtured, protected, cared for, and loved

Fantasies of conquest and being respected or even "worshiped" are very common with you in areas of sex, work, and social life. Sometimes you actually believe you are worshiped. These are powerful delusions, but they *are* delusions. It is impossible to control all the situations and people you come in contact with.

Even when you do succeed in getting people to comply, they only do it out of fear.

Respect is something you crave and demand from others, but it is also something you don't really understand. Someone who fears you doesn't necessarily respect you. Nor is respect something you deserve just because you happen to be walking on the planet. *Respect* means "high regard, or esteem." Therefore, respect must be earned over time through consistent, fair-minded, dedicated, compassionate behavior. Nothing else is "respect-able."

Given this definition of respect, the chances are good that not many people have ever truly respected you in your entire life. This may be hard news to swallow, but it is important for you to understand in order to gain genuine respect in the future.

Genuine Respect

➤ Name three people who you believe genuinely respect you. Do not include people who are afraid of you, who bow to your will out of self-protection but despise you in their hearts. List only people whose respect you have earned through consistent, fair-minded, compassionate thoughts, words, and actions. List only those who truly find you *respectable*. After each name, describe why you think this person respects you. If you can't name three people, name as many as you can.

Facilitator Note
The word *respect* comes from Latin and means "to look back at, to regard or consider."

Name of person	Reason you think this person respects you
1. _____	_____
	_____
	_____
2. _____	_____
	_____
	_____
3. _____	_____
	_____
	_____

Correcting Your Use of Power to Control

Have you ever wondered why you're so angry all the time? Have you noticed that other criminals—the people you hang out with, do crime with, or serve time with—are also very angry people? There are many reasons for your anger, but one of the main ones is the thinking pattern called use of power to control.

Trying to control everyone and everything all the time takes a lot of energy. A *whole* lot of energy. It's really hard work. Not only that, it's impossible! You can't control anyone or anything except your own thinking and behavior, so it's doomed to fail.

Think about it for a moment. Here you have a task (using power to control others) that you have devoted much of your life to and which is draining and frustrating and guaranteed to fail. No wonder you're angry all the time!

This anger may be expressed outright or may be just boiling beneath the surface, flashing out at unpredictable times. Much of your anger (and one of the reasons you try to use power to control) is your fear of being dissed, put down, humiliated. Your reaction to a perceived putdown is anger to reestablish control. But since you're always trying to control and never really succeeding for any length of time, you're almost always feeling put down. That's why when things happen to you that don't fit with your immediate desires, you see it as some form of disrespect. This leads to a near-constant state of anger and almost always trying to gain the upper hand through intimidation or undermining of others.

You can't control anyone or anything except your own thinking and behavior.

It's a vicious circle: attempts to control lead to perceived disrespect, which leads to anger, which puts you in the zero state, which leads to more attempts to control to get out of the zero state.

Figure 13
THE VICIOUS CIRCLE

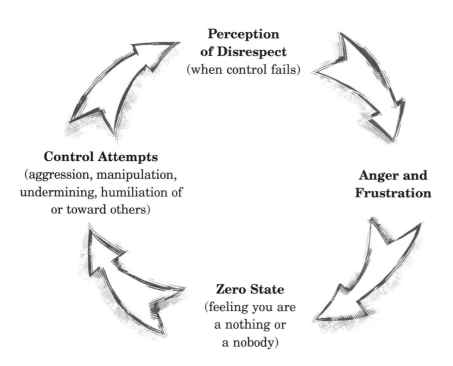

Perception of Disrespect
(when control fails)

Anger and Frustration

Zero State
(feeling you are a nothing or a nobody)

Control Attempts
(aggression, manipulation, undermining, humiliation of or toward others)

The only way out of this vicious circle is to learn to manage your anger and step away from the need to control. The truth is, you can control very little of your environment. You do not have the right or the ability to control others. Again, to dominate others is not to lead them; to frighten others is not to have their respect.

Zero-State Defenses

➤ In what circumstances do you feel especially powerless?
List them and then explain how you use power to control
to try to escape that feeling.

Situations when you feel powerless	How you use power to control
1. _____	_____
_____	_____
_____	_____
_____	_____
2. _____	_____
_____	_____
_____	_____
3. _____	_____
_____	_____
_____	_____

Using Power to Control

➤ Identify three ways that you use power to control others.

1. _____

2. _____

3. _____

➤ Check with your peers in the group. Ask them to identify three ways to control people that they have seen you use and that are different from the three you listed above.

1. _____

2. _____

3. _____

➤ *Power plays* are more indirect forms of aggression. Here are some examples of power plays:

- walking out of a room in the middle of a disagreement

- refusing to hear what someone has to say to you

- getting people to be angry at others as a way to support you

Now give three examples of power plays you have used.

1. _____

2. _____

3. _____

Letting Go of Control of Others

For one day this week, list every situation when you thought about controlling or tried to control someone else. Then put yourself in that person's place and imagine what you'd think and feel if you were him or her. If necessary, complete this exercise in a notebook.

➤ What was the situation?

_____

If I were him or her, I would

_____

_____

➤ What was the situation?

_____

If I were him or her, I would

_____

_____

➤ What self-talk would help to interrupt the urge to control others?

_____

_____

Real Feelings of Anger

Anger is normal. Everybody feels anger from time to time. As a criminal thinker, however, you feel something that is often not even real anger. Rather, it is something you show to others as a threat to try to control them. When you do experience real anger, however, you can quickly lose control of it and become very destructive.

➤ List three recent situations when you were angry. If you think it was a real feeling of anger, place an **X** under "real." If you showed anger just to intimidate someone, place an **X** under "show."

Situation   Real   Show

1. _____ _____ _____

   _____

   _____

2. _____ _____ _____

   _____

   _____

3. _____ _____ _____

   _____

   _____

Facilitator Note

Participants tend to think their own anger is always real; they are not practiced in making the distinction between real emotion and a dispassionate show of fake emotion for the purpose of manipulation. They are much more capable of seeing the lack of authenticity in the anger shown by their peers. If a participant lists all his anger as real, it may be valuable to have him get the feedback of his peers on the subject.

➤ What is it about the situations you marked "real" that make you think they were examples of genuine emotion?

_____

_____

_____

_____

➤ What is it about the situations you marked "show" that make you think your anger was just a way of manipulating others?

_____

_____

_____

_____

Below are four ways you can interrupt genuine anger before it leads you to do something stupid and destructive.

1. Tell yourself you can't afford to be angry.

2. Remind yourself how anger has gotten you into trouble in the past.

3. Ask yourself, Am I expecting too much in this situation? Can I cut everyone a little slack?

4. Ask yourself, What did I contribute to the situation to add to the conflict?

➤ List four more ideas on how you can interrupt your anger with your thinking before it gets you in trouble.

1. _____

2. _____

3. _____

4. _____

Facilitator Note
The *Socialization* module has an entire section on dealing with anger.

 EXERCISE **46** EXERCISE

Keeping an Anger Log

➤ Choose one day within the last seven days. List every time you became angry or started to become angry on that day.

1. _____

2. _____

3. _____

4. _____

5. _____

6. _____

7. _____

➤ What did you do? What were your other options? Which options were healthy and why? If necessary, complete this exercise in a notebook.

1. _____

2. _____

3. _____

4. _____

5. _____

6. _____

7. _____

➤ Of the anger situations you listed above, name three where you showed anger to manipulate and control even though you didn't really *feel* anger. (If you're not sure whether you really felt it, list that example here.)

1. _____

2. _____

3. _____

Seek Excitement First

One of the criminal thinking patterns that gets you into trouble the quickest is **seek excitement first.** The thoughts that urge you to seek excitement first keep you uninterested in a lot of responsible behavior. Here are some of the features of this type of thinking:

- You can't tolerate boredom.

- You can't stand being alone for more than short periods of time.

- You can't stay at a task (or a job) for long periods of time.

- You avoid obligations because they're too dull— they get in the way of your excitement.

- You seek excitement (especially through crime, drugs, and sex) on the spur of the moment. You live for today.

- Your thoughts of excitement are so powerful, they tend to push away any thoughts about consequences or what your conscience tells you.

- You think you're "nobody's sucker" when it comes to *responsible* living, but you're an easy mark to the *irresponsible* suggestions of others.

It's easy to see why you have probably found it difficult to hold on to a job for very long. One of the main reasons you struggle to hold a job is your desire to seek excitement first. You think:

- "This is too boring. I can't stand to do the same stuff over and over."

- "I can quit this job and get another that's more interesting."

- "I'm not a slug like the others at this job."

Facilitator Note

One major way "seek excitement first" thinking manifests is in how criminals approach relationships with the opposite sex. Relationships are pursued for the thrill of the chase, not for emotional fulfillment through caring and intimacy. Once the chase is over and the criminal has achieved what he sought— sexual release, power, or the humiliation of another— he moves on. See "Sexual Ownership Stance" on page 168.

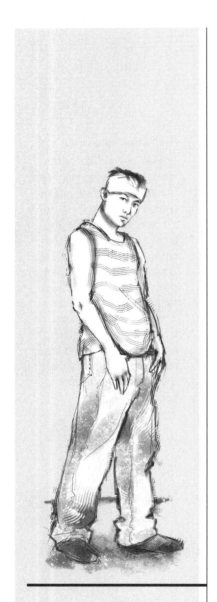

The decision to commit the criminal act is usually impulsive.

The problem is, *no* job is exciting enough for you. You move from one job to another chasing something that probably doesn't exist. And that leads you right to criminal behavior.

As we discussed earlier in this workbook, while you may have many criminal thoughts throughout the day, the decision to commit the criminal act is usually *impulsive*. That means the idea to commit the crime enters your head and you say to yourself something like, "Yeah, let's go for it." You feel the rush of adrenaline pumping in your veins, and you do the crime—sometimes without thinking about the consequences for yourself or others.

Later, when the excitement wears off and you face consequences, you use excuses and rationalizations to justify your behavior to yourself and others: "It was really *his* fault." "She shouldn't have dressed that way." "I did it because my old man beat me when I was a kid." When the consequences *really* come down hard, you may go into zero state.

Correcting "Seek Excitement First" Thinking

Responsible action is difficult for you. You're simply not used to it. Saying no to excitement will take some work. One way to change your "seek excitement first" thinking is to try to think "as if"—that is, practice thinking about doing the responsible thing even when it feels strange or uncomfortable or boring. Then follow through with action.

If you think and act as if you were responsible, eventually it will become a habit. In the end, you will *be* responsible—and receive the rewards of responsible living. These rewards are much greater than you think they are right now.

When is the right moment to practice thinking "as if"? It's when you begin to feel the surge of excitement you get from thinking about risky, irresponsible behavior. This feeling is called criminal excitement.

Criminal Excitement

Crime can be addictive. Just as you can be addicted to alcohol or other drugs, you also can be addicted to criminal excitement. Here are some examples of acting in criminal excitement:

- You have $30 for groceries, enough to get what you need, but you decide to shoplift the food just for kicks.

- You see a car idling in a parking lot, and you jump in and go for a joy ride.

Some of the things you do for criminal excitement aren't crimes, but they reinforce the "seek excitement first" thinking pattern. Here are some examples of these:

- trash talking on the basketball court—really trying to push the other guy to the edge

- "playing the dozens"—and getting nastier and nastier

- telling old criminal "war stories" to relive the rush of excitement

➤ List three examples of criminal excitement, even if you didn't actually end up committing a crime at the time. These are things you did mainly to get a rush.

1. _____

_____

2. _____

_____

3. _____

_____

➤ What thoughts went through your head at the time of these experiences? List one thought for each example you gave.

1. _____

_____

2. _____

_____

3. _____

_____

➤ What obligations or responsibilities did you blow off to follow that excitement?

1. _____

2. _____

3. _____

Consequences of
"Seek Excitement First" Thinking

Because you tend to do only what brings immediate gratification and excitement, you have lost out on experiences
that have deeper meaning. You have missed chances to
grow, learn, and become a better person. You may have
turned your back on career possibilities, being with family,
or other opportunities.

➤ What goals or responsible experiences have you given up
or lost because they weren't exciting?

1. _____

2. _____

3. _____

➤ Describe what your life might look like if you had followed
through on some of those goals and experiences.

_____

_____

_____

_____

Taking on Obligations

There are two kinds of obligations that healthy, responsible people accept. They are

1. **Everyday obligations.** These are things people must do regularly, such as personal cleanliness, going to work or school, helping a friend or spouse or child, obeying laws. For most responsible people, these obligations are practically automatic, which means they do them every day without having to think too much about it.

2. **Moral obligations.** These are acts of goodwill, things people do simply because they think they should try to make the world better. They may not get anything out of it themselves beyond knowing that they acted decently. For responsible people, that's often enough. Examples of moral obligations are giving time or money to charities, religious organizations, or community projects.

➤ List some of your everyday obligations (the things you must do regularly).

_____

_____

_____

_____

_____

Obligation

An *obligation* is a duty, contract, promise, or responsibility that makes someone follow a certain course of action.

➤ How well did you meet these obligations this past week?

_____

_____

_____

_____

_____

➤ List two possible ways you can fulfill moral obligations this coming week.

1. _____

_____

2. _____

_____

If you think and act as if you were responsible, eventually it will become a habit. In the end, you will <u>be</u> responsible—and receive the rewards of responsible living.

Failure to Take Responsible Action

There are many ways you fail to take responsible action. Here are some examples:

- You make an excuse to quit a job because it's "too much of a hassle."

- You think, "There's no guarantee I'll get a good job anyway, so I'm quitting school."

- You decide, "I tried to be responsible and it didn't work out the way I wanted, so I won't make the mistake of trying again."

➤ List three times you failed to take responsible action this past week.

1. _____

2. _____

3. _____

➤ What were you thinking when you blew off the responsible action that you were called to do or had an opportunity to do?

_____

_____

_____

_____

EXERCISE 51 EXERCISE

Resisting Suggestibility

As we mentioned earlier, as a criminal, you like to think of yourself as nobody's sucker. And yet, your "seek excitement first" thinking makes you almost anyone's sucker—at least when it comes to suggestions on how to make a big score quick and easy or chase some form of criminal excitement. While you are well defended against the values and thinking patterns suggested by therapists and other responsible people, you're easily tempted by thoughts of criminal and other irresponsible activity. Because your thoughts tend to seek excitement first, you are often an easy mark for anyone offering a thrill of almost any kind.

To become less vulnerable, you must begin to do the following:

- avoid association with irresponsible (criminal and drug/alcohol-using) people

- choose to hang with responsible people

- listen to, think about, and act on healthy suggestions from responsible people

➤ Five situations follow. How would you respond responsibly to each of them? Your responses should be clear and specific to each situation.

Situation 1:

"That babe winked at you. Go check it out. Your woman won't find out."

Response:

_____

_____

Facilitator Note
Be realistic with participants. It's inevitable that they will encounter situations like those given in this exercise. The point is, what are they going to do when they do encounter these situations? They need to have a plan— one they have rehearsed beforehand in order to deal with these situations.

You are often an easy mark for anyone offering a thrill of almost any kind.

_____

_____

_____

Situation 2:

> *"You don't have to sell it or even look at it. Just get it to the right guy across town tomorrow night. An easy $100."*

Response:

_____

_____

_____

_____

Situation 3:

> *"This is a great scam. I've worked it three times—never came close to getting caught. Let me show you how it works."*

Response:

_____

_____

_____

_____

Situation 4:

> *"I happen to know they leave the back door unlocked in case their oldest kid at college might stop in, and they're going out of town tonight. Meet me here tomorrow night and let's go see if they have any good stuff."*

Response:

_____

_____

_____

_____

Situation 5:

> *"Let's stop in here for a quick beer—just one."*

Response:

_____

_____

_____

_____

Ownership Stance

Ownership-stance thinking gives you a distorted idea about what are your rights and your property and what are the rights and property of others. It's one of the big reasons you are locked up right now. This thinking allows you to violate others or their property. When you use ownership-stance thinking, you do not see the difference between things that belong to you and those that belong to others—maybe because you think *everything* belongs to you. It also leads you to see others as your property to control and do with as you please. Your ownership stance prevents you from realizing that other people are independent human beings who have their own dreams, goals, desires, and purpose. Ownership-stance thinking can therefore be summed up as follows:

- One-way property boundaries ("What's mine is mine, and what's yours is mine.")

- The idea that people are property ("She's mine, so she has to do as I say.")

Sexual Ownership Stance

One of the ways you think about people as your property is with your sexuality. You think the purpose of others is to provide for your life needs, including your sexual needs. Most likely, you fantasize often about controlling others sexually. To get sex, you will manipulate, con, intimidate, lie, use force, or you will buy sex with drugs or money. You do this because of your ownership-stance thinking: You think the people you are attracted to owe you sex, simply because you want it. Because you think they owe it to you, you think it's okay to get it any way you can.

Your ownership stance prevents you from realizing that other people are independent human beings.

Correcting Ownership-Stance Thinking

One of the first things you need to do to correct your ownership stance is to start thinking differently about your relationships with others. You will need to learn to see other people as equal human beings. They are separate from you and have their own rights and property. What they do is for them to decide, not you. What they own is theirs, not yours.

You do have a connection with the people who are in your life. A healthy life in recovery requires that you learn to understand that connection and keep it in balance. What is the nature of one human being's relationship to another?

Figure 14
THE CONTINUUM OF DEPENDENCY

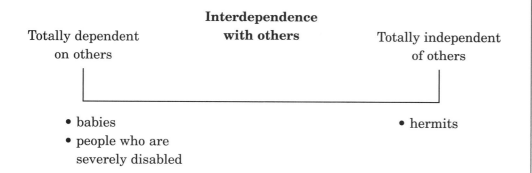

People relate to each other on a continuum of dependency. On one end you have those who are totally dependent on others to have life needs met, including what is necessary for survival. At the other end is complete independence of other human beings. Babies and people with very serious disabilities and illnesses who would not survive without the help of others are examples of totally dependent people. At the other end are hermits who live without any human contact whatsoever. Think about it: Who else is truly independent of all other human beings?

The truth is, we are all ***interdependent*** with one another. That means you need others and others need you. Healthy interdependence is a mix of dependent and independent thoughts and acts.

Sometimes in life you are more dependent on others; sometimes you are more independent of them. When you move too far toward one end of the continuum or the other, you become less healthy. You need to seek a balance. When adults are overly dependent on another person, something has gone wrong. Usually it means you are very sick, mentally or physically.

Extreme independence can also be a problem because we need connection with others. Extreme independence often shows itself in criminality: the disconnection from a healthy interdependence with others. Extreme independence means you cannot be close to anyone at any time. The opposite of this is ***intimacy.***

Victim stance, "good person" stance, use of power to control, "unique person" stance, ownership stance, and other criminal thinking patterns will either damage healthy relationships or prevent them from developing in the first place. This is because such relationships are based on lies, secrecy, and manipulation. To be intimate with someone, you must open yourself up to that person.

Interdependence

Interdependence in human relationships means sharing needs with others in a mutually agreed upon exchange. In its most basic form, it's like the old saying "You scratch my back and I'll scratch yours." But it really means much more than that. In a deeper sense, interdependence means living in a healthy way in which you give to and receive from your spouse or partner, family, community, society, and nature so that *most* life needs for you and for others around you can be met *most* of the time.

Intimacy

Intimacy is interdependent closeness with another. It requires honest sharing and a desire for the good of the other person.

Sexual fantasy that involves exploitation, an example of ownership-stance thinking and "seek excitement first" thinking, is a step backward in your efforts to recover from addiction and criminality. It defeats the possibility of intimacy.

Obsessing about whether you are getting "respect" or "disrespect" from others also holds you back in your recovery because it's about separating yourself out from others. The ownership stance involves thinking that other people exist to tell you what you want to hear or to make you feel about yourself the way you want to feel. In this way, other people become "things," property to you.

Finally, to change your ownership-stance thinking, you need to learn that property rights go two ways, not just one. You think that once you take something, it's yours. It's not. Just because you took it from someone doesn't mean it now belongs to you. In the same sense, you do not own things you have tricked someone into giving you through lies, threats, or empty promises.

The only things you own in life are your own thoughts and character and the material things you have earned through responsible effort.

Character vs. Reputation

Character is about your moral strength. It comes from finding the best qualities inside yourself, believing in them, and showing them every day in your behavior. Character is something you learn about yourself and then act on no matter what others may think.

Reputation is only about the image you try to get *others* to believe in. Most of the time, your reputation is just a con. It's your attempt to make others—and yourself—believe you are something that you're not.

"Be more concerned about your character than your reputation, because your character is what you really are, while your reputation is merely what others think you are."

—John Wooden, legendary UCLA basketball coach

Ownership Stance in Relationships

➤ List people on your visiting list or the people you call or write to.

1. _____

2. _____

3. _____

4. _____

5. _____

6. _____

➤ Look honestly at this list. In each case, what is the relationship based on, true caring or just getting someone to send you money or gifts?

1. _____

2. _____

3. _____

4. _____

5. _____

6. _____

Having Your Way

➤ List three ways in which you tried to have things your way during the past week.

1. _____

2. _____

3. _____

➤ How might you have violated the rights of others when you did those things?

1. _____

2. _____

3. _____

➤ How were the things you did examples of ownership-stance thinking?

_____

_____

_____

_____

_____

Two-Way Property Boundaries

As an example of how he was really a decent guy ("good person" stance), an inmate told a story about how, when his girlfriend brought home the money from her welfare check, he let her keep $50 of it to go buy herself something nice at Wal-Mart.

➤ How is this also an example of ownership-stance criminal thinking?

_____

_____

_____

➤ List six pieces of property in your cell that you think belong to you.

1. _____

2. _____

3. _____

4. _____

5. _____

6. _____

➤ How did you get these things?

_____

_____

_____

➤ What would you think if someone stole these things or conned you out of them?

_____

_____

_____

◼

If you have not already done so, you are now ready to start identifying the criminal thinking patterns you use and adding them to your Thinking Reports. You can also begin identifying different, healthier alternative thoughts. Both your criminal thinking patterns and alternative thoughts can be added to your worksheet on page 63.

Facilitator Note
Make sure participants go back to exercise 9b on page 63 and complete the criminal thinking patterns and alternative thoughts parts of their Thinking Report.

Conclusion of Parts 1–3

Congratulations. You have just completed your first workbook of the *Criminal and Addictive Thinking* module. In this first workbook, you've learned some big concepts. You've learned mapmaking, the importance of dealing honestly with your criminal and addiction history, how to fill out a Thinking Report, the different types of thinking distortions, and criminal thinking patterns. This workbook is valuable, so don't throw it away and rely on your memory. It contains information that will be referred back to in the second workbook and throughout this whole *A New Direction* curriculum. Also, it's really your own private journal of your recovery process. The material contained in this workbook will be helpful for you in your new crime-free, drug-free lifestyle. Now it's time to move on to parts 4–6 in the second workbook. Your facilitator will now give you the second workbook, if you don't have it already.

■　■　■

Facilitator Note
Remind participants to keep their first workbook and bring it to the next class session.

Facilitator Note

This is the close of the first workbook, sections 1–3, of the *Criminal and Addictive Thinking* module. You may wish to take some time to review with participants all that has been covered in this first workbook. Now is also a good time to hand out the second workbook, sections 4–6, to participants. Your facilitator guide includes the contents of both participant workbooks.

At the start of their second workbook, participants will be asked to write information from exercise 9b to page 179 in that workbook. For this reason, it's important that participants **hold on to their first workbook** and bring it to the next class session. (Another option would be to begin the second workbook now.) Even after participants have transferred exercise 9b to the second workbook, encourage them not to discard the first workbook. It can be used as a handy reference tool when dealing with issues found in the second workbook of this module. Essentially, the first workbook is a journal of their recovery process. It's an invaluable tool that they can use throughout this entire *A New Direction* curriculum.

Getting Started on Workbook 2

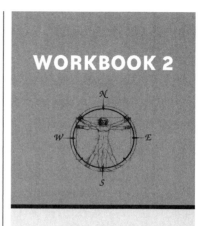

Welcome to the second workbook of this Criminal and Addictive Thinking module. Here you will learn all about how criminal and addictive thinking patterns reinforce each other, how core beliefs lead to thinking and behavior, the progression of criminal development and recovery, the progression of addiction development and recovery, and criminal and addictive tactics. It's a lot of information to cover, but it's all essential for your recovery from a life of crime and abuse of alcohol and other drugs.

Before we get started, let's quickly review the Thinking Report, a tool you have been using to better understand your thinking and to develop new, healthy patterns of thinking.

A Thinking Report is a way for you to practice thinking about your thinking, your core beliefs, and your behavior so you change them. Thinking Reports are a very important tool in helping you learn how to read your inner map. Knowing how to think about your own thinking is the most important basic skill you need to create a new successful thought map.

The seven main parts of the Thinking Report are

1. The **Event**—what exactly happened to begin the chain of thoughts, feelings, and behaviors or potential behaviors.

2. Your **Thoughts**—what popped into your mind when the event occurred.

3. Your **Feelings**—the emotions or other sensations that resulted from your thoughts about the event.

4. Your **Behavior**—your actions in response to the event as directed by your thoughts and reinforced by your feelings.

5. Your **Core Beliefs**—the assumptions you make about the world, others, and yourself.

6. Possible **Alternative Thoughts**—healthier thoughts that are different from your first, automatic thoughts and that could lead to a more positive outcome.

7. Possible **Alternative Behaviors**—what you could do based on your alternative thoughts.

In Thinking Reports, you are also asked to identify any Thinking Distortions, Thinking Patterns, and Tactics you use.

- Thinking Distortions were discussed in part 3 of the first workbook. They are consistently inaccurate and biased ways that people use to look at themselves, others, and the world.

- Thinking Patterns, discussed in parts 3 and 4, are habits of thought. Criminal and Addictive Thinking Patterns are thinking problems that have led to behavior problems in your life.

- Tactics, discussed in part 6, are habits of behavior that result from your thinking patterns and core beliefs.

Now, turn back to page 63 of workbook 1 and write your answers from that Thinking Report here. We'll be referring to those answers later in this workbook. As you copy the sections from the Thinking Report that you've filled out so far, pay attention to any areas that may still be confusing for you and then discuss these in group or with your therapist. Remember, learning how to replace unsuccessful patterns of thinking with rational choices will, over time, create new patterns and lead you to a happier, healthier, more free way of life.

Facilitator Note

Allow enough time for participants to transfer their answers from exercise 9b on page 63 of the first workbook to this introductory exercise. It will be referred to later in this workbook and it's important that it contains the event they noted early on in this module.

Thinking Report for Exercise 9b (continued)

Thinking Report

1. Event _____

_____

2. Thoughts _____

_____

3. Feelings _____

_____

4. Behavior _____

_____

5. Can you identify a core belief? _____

_____

6. Alternative thoughts _____

_____

7. Alternative behavior _____

_____

Thinking distortions _____

Thinking patterns _____

Tactics _____

Learning to Think about Your Thinking

ADDICTIVE THINKING PATTERNS AND CORE BELIEFS

As an addict, you have unhealthy thinking patterns that take you back to using time and again. As you continue to better understand how and why you think the way you do, you can begin to make the kinds of changes that will lead you to recovery.

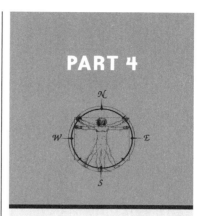

PART 4

A NEW DIRECTION

A Cognitive-Behavioral Treatment Curriculum

Facilitator Note

You may choose to show the *Criminal & Addictive Behavior: Tactics* video at this time. It shows the link between addictive and criminal thinking, common criminal tactics that are used and why they don't work, and how to make positive life changes.

Addictive Thinking Patterns

Addictive thinking patterns are very similar to criminal thinking patterns. In most cases, the only differences are in degree or in the particular direction the thinking takes. Remember the definition of criminal thinking patterns? *Criminal thinking patterns* are ways of thinking that say it is okay to violate others or the property of others.

The definition of addictive thinking patterns is similar: *Addictive thinking patterns* are ways of thinking that say it is okay to use as much drugs and alcohol as you want, as often as you want, and to do whatever you need to do to get them.

Thoughts that suggest, justify, or promote getting drunk and high no matter what the consequences to you or to others will most likely fit into one or more of the addictive thinking patterns categories.

Here are the addictive thinking patterns we've identified:

- self-pity stance
- "good person" stance
- "unique person" stance
- fear of exposure
- lack-of-time perspective
- selective effort
- use of deceit to control
- seek pleasure first
- ownership stance

*Addiction is a **thinking** problem*
*before it becomes a **drinking** problem.*

Denial

The main feature of addictive thinking is **denial.** Denial for the addict and alcoholic refers to the ability to contradict obvious facts, to turn the truth inside out, to look directly at *down* and to believe, with all your heart and mind, that it is really *up.*

One of the interesting features of denial is that you can often see in others what you can't see in yourself. Therefore, you may say something like, "Poor Pete. What a fool. He keeps drinking until he passes out, gets beat up, and rolled. What a chump." You can clearly see how pathetic Pete's situation is. What you can't see is how pathetic your own situation can be. You can't see how your alcohol or other drug use has gotten you in so much trouble that you've lost just about everything. Now you're incarcerated, probably not for the first time.

You haven't been able to see the truth about your own alcohol or other drug use because of your denial. To see that truth would mean you'd have to try recovery. It would mean you'd have to stop using. And that is what your addictive thinking calls you to deny—anything that would suggest you need to stop using.

> **Denial**
>
> *Denial* is used by addicts and alcoholics to keep themselves unaware of the harmful consequences of their use. Though addicts and alcoholics often lie to get what they want, denial is not about lying to others. Denial is a trick the addict's mind plays on itself to excuse the use of alcohol or other drugs no matter what harm it does.

Self-Obsession

As an addict, you are pleasure-centered and self-centered. That means your thoughts focus on whether or not you feel good. If you don't feel good, you become preoccupied with what you can do to make yourself feel good again as soon as possible. You had a powerful pleasure experience with drugs or alcohol (or with sex or gambling or eating or anything else people get addicted to) when you first used, and your mind became obsessed with repeating that

Denial is not a river in Egypt.

experience. When you feel bad, all you can think about is how to get drugs (alcohol, sex, and so on) so you will feel like you felt that first time you experienced them.

Because you are obsessed with feeling good, you tend to think only about your own wants and needs. Only after your wants and needs are met (for the moment, at least) are you able to consider the wants and needs of others.

Irrational Thinking

Because your thinking is driven by the obsession to feel good, it becomes *irrational*. Irrational thoughts lead to out-of-whack emotions and irrational behavior.

As an addict, you often use irrational thinking because you are not looking to find the truth. You are only looking to justify and excuse your single-minded search for the high. That is why your logic usually goes around in circles, even when it may seem to make sense on the surface.

Irrational thinking is thinking that is inconsistent with the facts. It contradicts itself and is confused, disorderly, and distorted. Irrational thinking does not use reason to find the truth; it makes arguments to try to prove a lie.

The Addict's Logic

A man is sitting at a bar. He is drunk. It is the tenth day in a row he has gone into the bar, sat on the same stool, and drunk until he nearly passed out.

"Why do you drink so much?" the bartender finally asks him.

"I drink because my wife doesn't understand me," replies the drunk.

"What doesn't she understand?" asks the bartender.

"She doesn't understand why I drink so much," says the man.

Why Do You Use?

➤ So why *do* you drink or use drugs? List five of your reasons—your excuses and rationalizations—for getting high. List the things you tell yourself and the things you tell others. Start each sentence with "I use drugs because . . ." or "I drink alcohol because . . ." Leave line 6 blank.

1. _____

2. _____

3. _____

4. _____

5. _____

6. _____

Now that you have listed the top five reasons you *think* you use alcohol or other drugs, here's the real reason:

You use alcohol or other drugs because you're a drug addict or an alcoholic.

➤ Now go back to your list of reasons for using and write the real reason on line 6: *I use drugs [or alcohol] because I'm a drug addict [or an alcoholic].*

Rational or Irrational Thinking?

Again, irrational thinking is confused or distorted thinking that contradicts the hard facts. Identify the following thoughts as either rational or irrational.

➤ Circle **R** for *rational* and **I** for *irrational.*

R **I** "Insurance pays for stuff that gets ripped off, so nobody really gets hurt."

R I "I'm really disappointed when I make a mistake and people get down on me."

R I "These homework assignments are really a pain to do."

R **I** "My therapist is always singling me out. She hates me and is out to make my time miserable."

R **I** "The therapists and administrators get paid a bonus for every one of us that gets kicked out of treatment."

R I "It's really a shame things didn't work out better than they did."

R **I** "I can't believe I relapsed. Face it—I'm just a loser."

R **I** "I'm better than just about everybody in so many ways."

R I "Damn! I wanted to play some hoops. I wish it wasn't raining."

Facilitator Note

The correct answers for exercise 56 are highlighted.

The purpose of this exercise is for participants to recognize their rational and irrational thinking.

R   I   "Flunking that class was a huge disappointment."

R   I   "They left it lying out in their yard. I found it. Now it's mine."

R   I   "I won't get caught next time because I won't make the same mistake I made before."

R   I   "Most women like forced sex."

R   I   "Some people have it easier in life than other people."

R   I   "Just because others get messed up by drugs doesn't mean I can't handle it. I'm tougher than they are."

R   I   "Listening to that music is really annoying."

R   I   "I wish I could have had the visit today."

R   I   "The therapists in this program love it when we fail."

R   I   "Trying to change my thinking is a lot of work."

R   I   "I've ruined everything I've touched in my life."

R   I   "If she didn't like getting hit, she wouldn't have come back home."

R   I   "Life isn't always fair."

Self-Pity Stance

As an addict, you have your own version of the victim-stance criminal thinking pattern. It's called the **self-pity stance.** You think the world is out to get you, that you're just a victim of bad luck. You have a hard time taking responsibility for what happens to you. You see yourself as the victim. In fact, if you're really pushed, you'd likely accept any explanation for how miserable and screwed up your life can be—as long as that explanation doesn't point a finger at your drug or alcohol use.

That *is* insane thinking. But it's not the result of mental illness—it's the result of your addiction to alcohol or other drugs.

"Poor me. Poor me. Poor me. Pour me . . . a drink."

—Recovery saying

EXERCISE **57** EXERCISE

Identifying Self-Pity Thinking

Self-pity thinking is one important way you justify your use of alcohol or other drugs. The following thoughts are examples of the self-pity stance:

- "I grew up in a tough neighborhood. I had to fight for survival. Having a hit or two now and then is the least I deserve for all I went through."

- "My dad was a drunk and my mom shot heroin. It's not my fault I use."

- "When I was in school, I always got punished for stuff I didn't do. Life's always been unfair to me."

➤ List three self-pitying thoughts you had last week.

1. _____

2. _____

3. _____

➤ Explain how your self-pity stance has set you up to use in the past.

_____

_____

_____

"Good Person" Stance

Despite all the things you've messed up and all the times you've let yourself and other people down, you still think you're a decent person. As an addictive thinker, you use four main strategies to create and maintain the illusion that you are essentially a good person, no matter what. They are the same strategies you use as a criminal thinker, only you also use them to justify your chemical use. These strategies are

- sentimentality

- selective memory

- excuses and rationalizations

- false comparisons and self-serving definitions

Despite all the things you've messed up, you still think you're a decent person.

You use these strategies to avoid thinking about yourself realistically. If you saw yourself clearly and realistically, it would be obvious even to you how drugs or alcohol have messed up your life and led you to hurt yourself and others. The purpose of "good person" stance thinking, like all other addictive thinking patterns, is to justify your continued use.

As an addictive thinker using the "good person" stance, you focus on the good things you've done and ignore the harm. You get **sentimental** about your mother but forget the times you lied to her or stole from her. Or you talk about how much your kids mean to you, even though you can't remember their birthdays. Or you try to make yourself look good by continually pointing out that someone else is worse than you. You say, "At least I'm not a crack head," or "I'm no gutter drunk like that guy." You believe in an addictive hierarchy just like you believe in a criminal hierarchy. The idea that some drugs are somehow "better" than other drugs, however, is delusional. They all do the same thing to your brain in the end—they hijack it. And they'll all kill you, sooner or later.

<table>
<tr><td>**Sentimentality**</td></tr>
<tr><td>*Sentimentality* is viewing your motives and intentions as always "good" on some level.</td></tr>
</table>

EXERCISE **58** EXERCISE

Can "Good" People Use Alcohol or Other Drugs?

➤ How does your view of yourself as a good person help you justify your use of alcohol or other drugs?

_____

_____

_____

Your Hierarchy of Drug Use

➤ List your hierarchy of drugs in order, from the "best" to the worst/most degrading. (Remember, alcohol *is* a drug.)

1. _____

2. _____

3. _____

4. _____

5. _____

6. _____

Facilitator Note

The drugs participants listed at the top—the so-called best drugs—will invariably be their drugs of choice. Ultimately, of course, it's just an excuse to use what they want to use. By putting some drugs low on the hierarchy, addicts psychologically elevate use of the drugs they prefer into the range of near-acceptability.

➤ What makes drugs 1 and 2 better drugs to use?

_____

_____

_____

_____

_____

➤ What makes drugs 5 and 6 worse drugs to use?

_____

_____

_____

_____

➤ How do you use your hierarchy of drugs to justify your own chemical use?

_____

_____

_____

_____

Facilitator Note

It is important to follow up exercise 59 with a thorough discussion of why the hierarchy of drugs is insane thinking designed only to justify continued chemical use. In essence, the hierarchy has no purpose other than to rationalize the use of one's drug of choice by setting up false comparisons.

"Unique Person" Stance

As an addictive thinker, you like to see yourself as different and special. You also tend to romanticize yourself. You may see yourself as a mysterious, adventurous, or tragic figure, like a pirate or an old-west cowboy or a gangster or some other super-bad, super-tough character.

You also think you are always right and have great difficulty admitting your mistakes. You are self-righteous. That means you will do whatever it takes to prove you are right—shouting down others, arguing over every little thing, bullying others into agreement or silence.

You use the **"unique person" stance** to feed your addiction. Perhaps you think your drug or alcohol use makes you especially cool—the hard drinker/smoker/snorter who can use more than anyone else and still be standing at the end of the night.

Your addiction is really the least unique thing about you. The truth is, you have a very common disease that has clear symptoms, familiar thought and behavior patterns, and predictable results. The story of your addiction is more or less the same as every other addict's story.

Here are examples of addictive thinking using the "unique person" stance:

- "I can drink anybody under the table."

- "Crack takes me places you can't even dream of."

- "I've smuggled more junk without getting caught than you'll ever see in your lifetime."

- "Don't tell me about what drugs do. I've forgotten more about chemicals than you'll ever know."

EXERCISE 60 EXERCISE

Your So-Called Unique Addiction

➤ List three things you have told yourself that were different about your alcohol or other drug use than anybody else's.

1. _____

_____

2. _____

_____

3. _____

_____

Facilitator Note

If possible, discuss exercise 60 in small groups. Have participants read the things they think are unique about their drug or alcohol use. Let other participants challenge that uniqueness.

Fear of Exposure

Just as your criminal thinking patterns are filled with many fears, so are your addictive thinking patterns. Here are four features of addictive **fear of exposure:**

- fear of self-knowledge

- excessive or inappropriate trust

- addict pride

- zero state

The first three represent a fear of change. You fear you'll be exposed as an addict or alcoholic and will have to stop using. So you hide your use or you flaunt it. You hide it so others won't know about your use and challenge it, or you flaunt it as a power move to make it seem like nothing can hurt you. Either way, you are afraid to take a good, hard look at your chemical use because you are afraid of changing your life in ways that might mean changing your use.

The zero state represents a fear that you cannot change, that you will get trapped in an intolerable condition of emptiness. In the zero state, you are frantic to change—though the *only* thing you really want to change is how bad you feel.

Fear of Self-Knowledge

You are afraid that if you really found out who you are, deep down, you might see that you are nothing. This is fear of the zero state that we discussed in criminal thinking patterns. You avoid self-knowledge to avoid looking at this fear—the fear that you might be worthless.

As an addict, you base trust on who might help you get high and who won't.

Excessive or Inappropriate Trust

As an addict, you base trust on who might help you get high and who won't. You tend to trust untrustworthy people who promise to help you get high. You tend to distrust trustworthy people who discourage or try to block your chemical use. Your trust is not based on facts or logic or even your own good sense of who is honest and who isn't.

Addict Pride

Most addicts have a sense of pride about their drug of choice. They think it is somehow better than other drugs. So a crack smoker might think heroin addicts are degraded for injecting their drug, while heroin addicts might say crack users are sick for how they can desperately chase the high for days on end in the worst conditions. Alcoholics may think their drug is better because it's legal, while ecstasy users think theirs is the coolest drug.

Zero State

As an addict, you also go into the zero state from time to time—the belief that you are worthless, nobody, empty inside. While your criminal thinking tends to use power over others as a way to escape the zero state, your addictive thinking tends to use deceit to control others or increased chemical use to find relief. In both cases, however, you will use both deceit and power to escape zero state, and you'll often use them together. As an addict *and* a criminal, you will use any of those strategies—whatever seems to work at the time.

As an addict, you tend to look on the dark side of things. You expect the worst and often see the worst in situations and others. Just as you use your expectation of an early death to justify your criminal behavior, you use the same dark thinking as an excuse to get high. You think, "If I'm doomed anyway, why not?"

You look on the dark side of things. You expect the worst and see the worst in situations and others.

Despite your thoughts of impending doom, when it comes to your chemical use, you also have an irrational belief that alcohol and other drugs will not have a harmful effect on your body and brain. You assume they won't have the same destructive results on your body that they have on everyone else's.

So either you *deny* the harm of chemical use or you *accept* it because you don't care, since you're doomed anyway.

Remember the continuum of fear you looked at in the section on criminal thinking patterns? It looks like this:

Figure 15
THE CONTINUUM OF FEAR

Too Afraid	Healthy Fear	No Fear
Has so many fears, many of them irrational, that he can't make a healthy decision.	Has rational fears that guide him to take care of himself and motivate him to make healthy decisions for change	Lacks rational fears—thinks he's infallible and invulnerable—and doesn't think he needs to make any changes. Thinks he's invincible (cannot be defeated or caught) and invisible at the same time.

Paranoia

Paranoia is a mental condition of extreme suspiciousness and lack of trust. When you are paranoid, you have an irrational belief that people are out to get you. You may think everyone is looking at you, talking about you behind your back, or plotting against you even though it is not true.

As an addict, you tend to live on both extremes of this continuum: either full of irrational fears or lacking the healthy fears that might protect you. One of the reasons you may be "too afraid" is that many mind-altering chemicals tend to cause ***paranoia*** in the user. Meth, angel dust, and marijuana are some of the drugs whose users have reported experiencing paranoia.

You also lack healthy fears that would keep you from harm, especially in regard to your chemical use. That is why you are willing to put some pill or powder you bought from a dealer you may not even know into your body. Because getting high is more important to you than your own physical safety, you are willing to believe exactly what the dealer tells you. You trust this even when you know the dealer to be a highly untrustworthy person! You trust this even when you know the drug has been cut, and you know what you have used to cut stuff yourself.

EXERCISE **61** EXERCISE

Risk Taking

➤ Give three examples of serious risks you have taken to get high.

1. _____

2. _____

3. _____

➤ Is there anything else in your life (besides chemicals) that is so attractive it would lead you to take such risks? If so, what is it?

_____

_____

_____

Facilitator Note
Offenders often will be suspicious of taking medications prescribed by a physician for real physical (including neurological) ailments. If you have participants who have resisted taking rigidly controlled dosages of prescribed medication for high blood pressure, depression, or psychosis because they distrust doctors, ask them to consider the extraordinary risks they willingly assume to get high. Ask them to think about the individuals of poor character into whose hands they will place their faith—and their lives—in order to get high.

Facilitator Note
Offenders will also take extraordinary risks for sex and thrills. As an additional part of this exercise, have participants detail the potential consequences of all these risks.

Lack-of-Time Perspective

Because getting high (feeling intense pleasure) is the most important thing in your life, you tend to live only in the present when you are high and only in the near future ("How can I get more soon?") when you are not high. This **lack-of-time perspective** is one feature of your thinking that denies the health damage and social consequences of using by blocking out thoughts of the long-term future.

Your lack-of-time perspective also shows up in how you get cause and effect mixed up. *Cause and effect* means that when you do A (cause), then B (effect) happens. For example, if you jump in a lake (cause), you will get wet (effect).

It seems pretty simple. But what about the following causes and effects?

- If you steal your girlfriend's money to buy drugs (cause), she will get angry and upset and nag you about your irresponsibility (effect).

- If you get drunk all the time (cause), you will lose your job (effect).

In the addict's deluded (reversed) version of cause and effect, the thinking goes like this:

- Because my girlfriend nags and gets angry all the time (cause), I get high (effect).

- Because they fire me from every job (cause), I drink (effect).

By reversing cause and effect in the moment, you fail to look at what happened in the past—that your chemical use created serious problems. You also can't see what will happen in the future—that more serious problems will be caused by continued use of alcohol and other drugs if you don't stop now. Your chemical use is not the *result* of your problems; it is the primary *cause* of them—past, present, and future.

Thinking about the Past and Future

➤ List three examples of when your use of alcohol or other drugs (cause) has led to negative consequences (effect).

1. _____

_____

2. _____

_____

3. _____

_____

➤ Imagine your life five years from now if you were to continue using alcohol or other drugs. What will it be like? What will *you* be like?

_____

_____

_____

_____

Selective Effort

As an addictive thinker, you will go to great trouble to get and use alcohol and other drugs. Just as you have plenty of energy when you need it for crime, you can go without food and sleep in your pursuit of getting high. However, when it comes to the day-to-day obligations of responsible living, you can't be bothered. You're too tired or too un-interested—or too busy getting high.

In part, this is because of your unwillingness to tolerate frustration. You often won't make the effort to try anything new or difficult because

1. If you fail, it might send you into the zero state.

2. You are afraid of all change, because growth and change threaten your using.

Your **selective effort** is part of the self-centeredness of your addictive thinking. You have the energy to fulfill your own pleasure desires, but not enough for others, including your children or other loved ones. You have the drive to score and use chemicals, but not to find and keep a job or finish school.

Codependence

Codependence is abandoning yourself—your own needs and growth and development opportunities—in order to give all your energies to taking care of someone else. Codependence is an unhealthy way of thinking and living.

Magical Thinking and Codependency

Selective effort is more than self-centeredness. It is also a feature of your magical thinking. You tend to think that somehow things will work out without you having to make any effort. You think that somehow the trouble you've gotten yourself into will just go away. This magical thinking probably followed you into treatment.

It is also often the result of the ***codependent*** thinking of others. Since you are generally unwilling to make an effort, you try to get other people to make the effort for you. You want them to clean up all the messes you create with your chemical abuse, to do the work (effort) that is your responsibility, and to take care of you.

It is not surprising that addicts and alcoholics seek out codependents and that codependents seek out addicts and alcoholics. It is a powerful attraction. It is also an unhealthy relationship because each helps the other continue the thinking and behavior that is most destructive for them. Over time, codependents and addicts/alcoholics will (1) make themselves and each other miserable, and (2) eventually destroy their own and each other's lives.

EXERCISE **63** EXERCISE

Identifying Your Selective Efforts

➤ What obligations and responsibilities have you blown off to use chemicals?

_____

_____

_____

_____

_____

_____

Facilitator Note
Relationships should be the number one answer here. For many, it will be their relationships with the women and children in their lives.

EXERCISE **64** EXERCISE

Naming Your Codependents

➤ List the codependents in your life by asking the following questions: Who sends you money? Who raises your kids? Who do you expect to take care of your business, the obligations and responsibilities you listed in exercise 63?

1. Name _____

   What do you expect of this person?

   _____

2. Name _____

   What do you expect of this person?

   _____

3. Name _____

   What do you expect of this person?

   _____

4. Name _____

   What do you expect of this person?

   _____

Use of Deceit to Control

Both criminal and addictive thinkers believe they need to control others and situations. Addictive thinking says it is okay to use chemicals. When people challenge you on this, you want to control them. You believe that if you can control others and situations, you can continue with your chemical abuse.

As a criminal, you try to control others mainly through power tactics. As an addict, you try to control others mainly through lies. Since you are both a criminal and an addict, you use a mixture of both power and deceit, with each feeding into the other.

Using deceit to control means you will lie, cheat, steal, tell half-truths, and beg to get and continue using alcohol or other drugs. Denial is one form of deception. It is deceiving yourself about the harm of your chemical use. As an addict, however, you are also willing to lie to others as much as necessary in order to keep using. This kind of lying is different from denial—it is aggressive, self-centered, and extremely damaging to all your relationships.

The addictive thinking that uses deceit to control takes three directions:

1. You tend to become defensive when challenged about your chemical use, or you tell half-truths or make empty promises about quitting.

2. You must always be right about everything, since being wrong threatens your illusion of control. Therefore, you argue frequently and exaggerate to "win" arguments.

3. You will use this controlling power of deceit to keep others off balance to avoid challenges to your chemical use and maintain your source of supply.

Who Have You Lied To?

As an addict, you will lie to anyone who might stand in the way of your getting or using alcohol or other drugs. Usually, these are the people closest to you: your spouse or significant other, kids, parents or grandparents, friends, neighbors, co-workers, and employers.

➤ Name five people you have lied to in order to get, use, or get away with using alcohol or other drugs. Then describe how the lies were designed to control that person's behavior so you could keep using.

Person you lied to	How did the lies you told control that person?
1. _____	_____
	_____
2. _____	_____
	_____
3. _____	_____
	_____
4. _____	_____
	_____
5. _____	_____
	_____

Facilitator Note

Most offenders will claim they tell the truth most of the time, failing to recognize the lying they do with half-truths and by omission. Participants need to significantly broaden their concept of what lying is.

The People Closest to You

➤ List the three most important people in your life. Then list three lies you told each of them in order to get, use, or get away with using alcohol or other drugs.

Name of person close to you: _____

Lies you told this person in order to use:

    1. _____

    2. _____

    3. _____

Name of person close to you: _____

Lies you told this person in order to use:

    1. _____

    2. _____

    3. _____

Name of person close to you: _____

Lies you told this person in order to use:

    1. _____

    2. _____

    3. _____

Facilitator Note

This will be a difficult assignment for participants since they might not want to admit that they've lied to someone they care about. If they have problems listing the lies, ask them about specific situations where their family members or friends got on their case. Did they end up lying to cover up?

➤ How did your lies give you control (even for a short time) over these people?

_____

_____

_____

➤ How did these and other lies affect your relationships with these people?

_____

_____

_____

➤ What does it mean to you that you are willing to lie to the people who are most important in your life so you can get high?

_____

_____

_____

Seek Pleasure First

As a criminal thinker, you tend to seek excitement first and worry about consequences later (if at all). This impulsiveness is also a part of your addictive thinking. As an addictive thinker, you tend to **seek pleasure first**—the pleasure of getting high. You will seek this pleasure without regard for the serious physical, mental, and legal consequences that result. Even after your body begins to build a tolerance to your drug(s) of choice and it becomes more and more difficult to find a good high, you continue to seek, out of habit and physical craving, the drug-induced pleasure you once felt.

Addiction is a powerful mental and physical habit, driven by your memories of pleasurable drug experiences, your body's craving for the drug, and your unwillingness to tolerate discomfort. That means that when you feel frustrated, bored, anxious, or uncomfortable, your first thought is to relieve that discomfort as quickly as possible, and the fastest way you know to do that is with chemicals. Once you get the idea that you need to get high, little can stand in your way. You'll generally do whatever you need to do to find and use alcohol or other drugs. This is called *obsession,* and "seek pleasure first" thinking is the way your mind feeds your obsession with getting high.

Obsession

An *obsession* is a powerful and persistent idea or feeling that demands almost all your attention.

One of the problems with your use of alcohol or other drugs and the thinking that leads you to seek pleasure first is that you identify happiness or feeling stress-free with being high.

A drug or alcohol high is a very temporary state.

Your body can't stand being intoxicated for long without breaking down. So when you are between highs or when your body develops *tolerance* and the high is less intense, it becomes very difficult for you to feel good. In this way, your "seek pleasure first" thinking actually leads you to more and more misery over time—and less and less pleasure. You become increasingly dissatisfied with everything and everybody, and you may find that even things that used to bring you joy no longer do.

Tolerance

Tolerance is the body's increasing resistance to the effects of a drug that results from frequent use over time.

 EXERCISE 67 EXERCISE

Seeking Pleasure First

➤ List the main ways that you seek pleasure first when you are feeling bad or stressed. Be sure to list the behaviors, including chemical use (listing the specific drugs you'd choose), that you use to try to cover up uncomfortable feelings.

1. _____

2. _____

3. _____

4. _____

5. _____

6. _____

Dealing with Discomfort

Discomfort is a temporary state. When you feel bad, it can seem as if you will feel this way forever. This is not true: Comfort and discomfort come and go in life all the time. Nobody can feel good all the time, and the bad feelings also will pass with time (except with certain illnesses, of course).

➤ When you feel uncomfortable, your mind turns to ways of feeling better immediately rather than working through the discomfort. List two situations that make you feel anxious, uneasy, angry, irritated, or uncomfortable in some way.

1. _____

2. _____

➤ When you are in such situations, what are the first three things you think of doing to make yourself feel better?

1. _____

2. _____

3. _____

➤ What if you didn't do anything to make yourself feel better in such situations? What could you do to work through your discomfort instead of trying to cover it up?

_____

_____

Facilitator Note

It is important that participants realize that discomfort is part of the recovery process. It cannot be avoided.

Ownership Stance

When you learned about criminal thinking, the **ownership stance** was summed up in two ideas:

- one-way property boundaries
  ("What's mine is mine, and what's yours is mine.")

- the idea that people are property
  ("She's mine, so she has to do as I say.")

With addictive thinking, this ownership stance and its disregard for the property rights of others comes from your obsession with getting high. Since you will do whatever it takes to feed your addiction, you mistakenly believe it is somehow okay for you to steal and to cheat others to get what you want most: drugs or alcohol. You also often treat others as if their purpose in life is to help you feel better—to get you drugs or alcohol, or provide you with sex, and to clean up the messes you make. This thinking turns people into property for you. It defeats the possibility of having a healthy relationship.

One of the ways you treat others as property is by expecting them to constantly behave in ways to better meet your needs. You have been unwilling, however, to make changes in yourself. You have decided somewhere along the road that the world should adjust to you rather than you adjusting to the world. That kind of ownership-stance thinking says the world is yours to use and violate in any way you wish to get what you want.

It's not hard to understand why people with this kind of thinking end up behind bars! Ownership-stance thinking separates you from others because you don't care about anyone else's real needs or rights. So you see, long before you were separated from society by being locking up, you had already separated yourself out from family, friends, and community with your ownership-stance thinking.

You have been unwilling to make changes in yourself.

The Property of Others

➤ List five things you stole to get drugs or alcohol.

1. _____

2. _____

3. _____

4. _____

5. _____

Facilitator Note
Examples might include
money, purses, and cars.
Ask them to be as specific
as possible in their answers.

➤ Describe some of the thoughts you had to justify stealing these things.

1. _____

2. _____

3. _____

➤ Why do you think it's okay for you to take the property of others but not okay for others to take your property?

_____

_____

_____

People Are Not Property

➤ Who are the people you used to help you get and use alcohol or other drugs? List three of them (by first name or initials only, if you choose). These are people you expect to provide excuses or to cover up for you. They are also friends, relatives, or acquaintances you have stolen from or ripped off in other ways (including dealers you bought drugs from and people you sold drugs to), and strangers you have cheated or robbed to buy drugs. (You may identify the strangers in any way that makes sense to you. For example, you could write, "The owner of the blue Buick" if, for example, you had stolen a CD player from a blue Buick in order to get money for drugs.)

Facilitator Note

Emphasize that treating people like property is never okay.

People you used	How you used them
1. _____	_____
	_____
	_____
2. _____	_____
	_____
	_____
3. _____	_____
	_____
	_____

➤ What would you have to do to live in a way that did not use others as if they were your property?

_____

_____

_____

_____

Changing Addictive Thinking

To review, addictive thinking patterns are ways of thinking that say it is okay to use drugs and alcohol whenever you want to and as much as you want to. These thinking patterns also give you the go-ahead to do whatever you need to do to get drugs and alcohol. The patterns justify getting drunk and high no matter what the consequences to yourself or to others.

Here are the main addictive thinking patterns:

- self-pity stance
- "good person" stance
- "unique person" stance
- fear of exposure
- lack-of-time perspective
- selective effort
- use of deceit to control
- seek pleasure first
- ownership stance

Facilitator Note
Addictive thinking patterns are dangerous because they attempt to justify using behavior.

Denial is the most important feature of addictive thinking. Denial is the way addicts and alcoholics keep themselves unaware of the terrible consequences of their use.

To change your addictive thinking patterns, you first need to learn to recognize the patterns as the thoughts happen. Second, you need to slow down, stop the rush to always feel good, and think for a moment. Because you liked the intensity of the high and how it made you feel, you tend to focus on the immediate pleasure but not the long-term pain.

This is the big lie that you have been telling yourself: that drugs bring you pleasure but have no consequences. The truth is, they probably played a big role in why you are locked up right now or have been locked up in the past.

 EXERCISE **71** EXERCISE

Becoming Aware of Your Addictive Thinking

Think back to the last time you really wanted to get high. It might have been last week, yesterday, or an hour ago. If necessary, complete this exercise in a notebook.

➤ What was the situation? Where were you and who were you with? What was being talked about? What did you hear, smell, see, or taste that you associated with getting high?

_____

_____

_____

_____

_____

➤ What did you feel in your body at the time? The physical symptoms of cravings vary with different people, so you need to learn what *your* symptoms are. For example, your stomach may have tightened up or you may have gotten the sweats. Perhaps your heart beat faster or you felt fatigued. Maybe your mouth began to water or got very dry. Describe exactly how you were feeling.

_____

_____

_____

➤ What was your emotional state? Again, it can be different for different people. You may have felt agitated or calm, sad, angry, frustrated, joyful, panicked, or bored. You may have felt many different things all at once. List them all.

_____

_____

➤ What were you thinking at the time? This may be the hardest to remember, but it's also the most important. You may have started thinking about drinking or about how to score something and then use it. Perhaps you tried to convince yourself to resist the urge. Be very specific in describing your thoughts.

_____

_____

_____

Here are the main
addictive thinking patterns:

- self-pity stance
- "good person" stance
- "unique person" stance
- fear of exposure
- lack-of-time perspective
- selective effort
- use of deceit to control
- seek pleasure first
- ownership stance

➤ List the addictive thinking patterns that you use the most.

1. _____

2. _____

3. _____

4. _____

Relapse Indicators

The thoughts and feelings you listed in exercise 71 can trigger cravings and cause relapse. (They will be discussed at much greater length in the Relapse Prevention module of this treatment program.) Think of them as danger signs along the roadway, such as "Bridge Out," "Beware Falling Rocks," or the flashing red lights of fire engines and ambulances. When you become aware of these relapse indicators, you need to, in a sense, slow down and pull over to the side of the road. You need to think hard about who you are and where you want to go before proceeding on in the same direction you're headed. When the signs say "Danger Ahead," there's danger ahead. When your relapse indicators come up, relapse isn't far away.

How Criminal and Addictive Thinking Patterns Reinforce Each Other

Criminal and addictive thinking patterns are not only similar, they also feed each other. Criminal thinking patterns will lead you to addictive thinking patterns and vice versa. This means that if you commit a crime, the thinking involved will likely lead you to use alcohol or other drugs. If you use drugs or alcohol, the thinking that convinces you to do that will quite possibly lead you back to criminal activity. You begin to think you are invincible and invisible again—nothing can stop you and you won't get caught because you're too careful and slick. (See figure 16 on page 218.)

Drugs and alcohol lower your inhibitions and increase your impulsivity. Inhibitions are thought patterns that hold you in check and prevent you from doing something. A value system that says it's wrong to steal is an inhibition against stealing. The ability to understand another person's pain is an inhibition against hurting others. A belief that drugs or alcohol and criminal behavior are ruining your life and hurting your loved ones can be an inhibition against relapse and committing crimes in the future.

You are short on healthy inhibitions to begin with.

But when you lower them by getting drunk or high, you become even more impulsive and self-destructive. The following exercises will help you see how your addiction and your criminality work together to mess up your life.

Facilitator Note
Figure 16 on page 218 illustrates how criminal and addictive thinking drive each other. The two go hand in hand.

Figure 16
HOW CRIMINAL AND ADDICTIVE THINKING DRIVE EACH OTHER

ADDICTIVE THINKING

Controls with Deceit
  manipulates with lies
  undermines and confuses
  passive-aggressive
  abusive
  cheats and cons

Self-Obsessed
  self is shameful
  self-pitying
  loner
  unique
  resentful

Irresponsible
  false promises
  sexually selfish
  impulsive
  unreliable
  denies facts
  ducks obligations

False Pride
  self is special
  grandiose
  sentimental
  cynical
  fear of death
  self is smarter
  intolerant

Pleasure Focused
  craves sensuality
  instant gratification
  lustful
  low discomfort tolerance

Rigid
  self-righteous
  defensive
  need to be right
  perfectionistic
  judgmental
  absolutist

CRIMINAL THINKING

Controls with Power
  manipulates with threats
  undermines and confuses
  intimidates
  abusive
  cheats and cons

Self-Centered
  self is nothing (zero)
  self is victim
  loner
  unique
  entitled

Irresponsible
  lack of effort
  sexually predatory
  impulsive
  unreliable
  distorts facts
  refuses obligations

Criminal Pride
  self is good person
  extremely high self-image
  sentimental
  cynical
  fear of humiliation
  self is tougher
  quick temper

Excitement Focused
  craves thrills
  instant gratification
  power hungry
  low boredom tolerance

Concrete
  self-righteous
  close-minded
  need to be on top
  perfectionistic
  all or nothing
  absolutist

Your Drug and Alcohol Crimes

➤ List some crimes you committed to get drunk or high.

_____

_____

_____

➤ List crimes you committed _while_ you were drunk or high.

_____

_____

_____

➤ Are there crimes you believe you might _not_ have committed if it weren't for your alcohol or drug use? List them.

_____

_____

_____

◼

If you have not already done so, you are now ready to start identifying the addictive thinking patterns and alternative thoughts and adding them to your Thinking Report on page 179.

Facilitator Note

This exercise is designed to get the participants thinking about how their drinking and using is linked to their criminal activity.

Participants can add their addictive thinking patterns and alternative thoughts to the Thinking Report on page 179 of their workbook.

Core Beliefs

Remember, core beliefs are those generalized beliefs or "rules" that are true throughout our thinking and applied to almost all situations. They are the very basic assumptions we make about the world, others, and ourselves. They are so automatic that we often don't even stop to think about them. Core beliefs make up what we believe about reality and our self-identity—what we hold as important or meaningful, and what options or choices we see as available to us.

Core beliefs are the thoughts behind our thinking.

They are the thoughts that lead us from "That person makes me mad" to "He deserves to be hit," or from "I like the looks of that car" to "Therefore it's okay for me to steal it." Or they are the thoughts behind the thinking that takes us from "I should never have to feel bad" to "Therefore it's all right to use alcohol or drugs because I deserve to feel good." Your beliefs determine how you justify and explain your behavior. They are the story you tell yourself and others that makes it okay for you to rob, steal, assault, and use alcohol and drugs despite the consequences to yourself and your relationships.

Not all your core beliefs are distorted. Some of them help to protect you. They also help you to consider the needs and safety of others. Healthy core beliefs don't cause harm to others—they don't create victims.

Identifying Your Core Beliefs

➤ Write down the first thing that comes to your mind:

Facilitator Note
By completing this exercise, participants will be working on identifying their own core beliefs.

1. The world is _____

2. Other people are _____

3. Other people should try to _____

4. I try to be _____

5. The world would be better if _____

    _____

6. The best way to get what you want is to _____

    _____

7. I deserve _____

    _____

8. If people try to stop me from getting what I want, then

    _____

    _____

"The Little Engine That Could"

Core beliefs are the thoughts behind your thinking. Remember the children's story called *The Little Engine That Could*? The story is about a small train engine that is asked to pull many freight cars filled with toys and candy across a mountain. The train's first engine had broken down and no other engines were willing to do the work. Though no one thought the little engine was powerful enough for the job, it volunteered to try. It started out by saying to itself, "I think I can. I think I can." It kept saying "I think I can" as it picked up speed and as it began the long, hard climb up the mountain. It continued to say it until it finally reached the top and could begin the easy trip down the other side.

What does this simple child's tale have to do with core beliefs? Let's work backward:

Question: What was the behavior?
Answer: Pulling the train over the mountain.

Question: What was the thought behind the behavior?
Answer: I think I can.

Question: What was the core belief behind the thought?
Answer: I believe that, with effort and determination, I can do more than others think I'm capable of doing.

Your core beliefs support your thinking, just like the rocks and earth underneath the ground support the world you live in. You don't see them, but they are there. You can also think of core beliefs as the framework of a big building—the girders and beams that make up the skeleton of the building—that you don't see but that keep the whole building from collapsing.

The same is true of your core beliefs. They are so automatic that we are often not even aware of their impact on our thinking and behavior. But by looking at your thinking distortions and criminal and addictive thinking, you can begin to identify which of your core beliefs cause harm to others—and to yourself.

Here are some examples of core beliefs.

View of the world:

- It's a dog-eat-dog world.
- Life is tough and then you die.
- The world should be just and fair.
- People get what they deserve out of life.

View of others:

- Everyone is out for themselves.
- Get them before they get you.
- Treat others as you'd want to be treated.
- Others are inferior to me.
- Others are here to meet my needs, or at least they should stay out of my way.
- If everyone else would get their act together, I would be fine.
- People are basically good.

View of self:

- I am above others and deserve respect at all times.

- Since I am special, I deserve special treatment.

- I can make a positive difference in people's lives.

- Rules aren't for me; I am entitled to break the rules.

- If people knew the real me, they would reject me.

- My feelings are always correct.

Based on your core beliefs, you develop certain strategies to make things go according to your thinking. But you—like most people—generally look at the world *through* your core beliefs. You seldom look *at* them. And you believe that everyone else in the world looks at things the way you do. For example, you probably think:

- Everybody in your situation would have done the things you did.

- Everybody uses because everybody in *your* world uses.

- If everybody had as hard a life as you, they'd commit crimes, too.

Sometimes things happen that go against what you believe are "just the way things are." When this is the case, you are much more likely to change or distort that information to fit what you already believe. Again, that's true for most people, not just criminals.

Criminals, however, have core beliefs that allow for and justify criminal behavior.

So when you believe it's a dog-eat-dog world and someone does something nice for you, you automatically think that person must be trying to con you. When people make you angry, you tell yourself you are justified in beating them up because "they asked for it" or "they should have known better" or "they simply got what they deserved."

A problem that many people, including criminals, have with their core beliefs is that they think everyone has the same core beliefs that they have. It's wrong to assume that our core beliefs are the same as everyone else's. Many of your life's conflicts happened because you tried to insist that everyone else shares your core beliefs. The world of your core beliefs is way too small. And that's one reason why your thought map has failed you: It doesn't tell you much about the larger world you live in. Your small, criminal core beliefs have kept you trapped in a small, criminal world.

One of the basic goals of treatment is to get you to look at, and question, some of your core beliefs. You need to look at the "rules" that you apply automatically across different situations. Doing so will cause you to react and behave in ways that create problems for yourself and others. As a result this examination is a very difficult thing to do.

How Core Beliefs Lead to Thinking and Behavior

➤ Write your current offense below in the far right-hand column. Then review your answers to the questions in exercise 73. Use those answers as a guide to the core beliefs that seem to have a connection to your current offense. List them below in the far left-hand column.

In the middle column, write a thought that could come out of each of the core beliefs that would lead to committing your current offense.

Core beliefs	Specific thoughts	
1. _____	_____	
_____	_____	
2. _____	_____	
_____	_____	_____
		current offense
		(behavior)
3. _____	_____	
_____	_____	

The crime is the behavior. It resulted from specific thoughts like the ones you described above. The thoughts came out of your core beliefs about the world, others, and yourself.

Exercise 73 helped you start to become aware of your core beliefs. It will take you much more time and effort to identify your basic beliefs and to challenge them. Seeing what kinds of issues come up again and again in your Thinking Reports and what your thoughts are leading up to in those situations can help your thinking become more deliberate and less reactive.

If you have not already done so, you are now ready to start identifying the core beliefs (the thoughts behind your thoughts) that operate behind your criminal and addictive thinking patterns and to start adding core beliefs to your Thinking Reports. You are also ready to begin trying to think of replacement core beliefs—new beliefs—that might work better for you in recovery. Adding new beliefs may lead you to healthier, more rewarding thoughts and outcomes. Add this information to your Thinking Report on page 179.

Facilitator Note
The participants should now be ready to add their core beliefs to the Thinking Report on page 179 of this workbook.

Facilitator Note
See page 228 for an optional exercise to learn about the core beliefs.

Optional Exercise

This optional "mental filter" exercise is best performed with a small group of people seated in a circle. This exercise can be easily altered to meet your own needs. Materials needed: several dozen coffee filters and markers. Label the filters with various basic core beliefs, such as

- Negative beliefs about [fill in the race, gender, or sexual orientation] people
- "It's a dog-eat-dog world."
- "Everybody's looking out for number one."
- "Life is supposed to be fair."
- "I am a man among men."
- "It's smart to do unto others before they do unto you."
- "The purpose of life is to get what you want."
- "I'm superior to others."
- "I'm inferior to others."

You may come up with other core beliefs during group discussions. After writing the core beliefs on the coffee filters, assign two or three filters to each group member. Tell the participants that core beliefs are like coffee-filled coffee filters for the brain—everything that happens to each of them, every bit of information that they take in about the world through their senses, passes through their core beliefs before it gets to the conscious brain and begins to make sense. What is contained in their core beliefs, then, plays a major role in how they interpret data—the quality, shadings, or "flavoring" of the information they take in—just as the coffee in a coffee filter changes the quality of the hot water passing through it. The thoughts they will think in response to external situations, therefore, are filtered through their core beliefs.

Ask each of the participants to memorize the core beliefs on their two or three filters and then to hold the filters to their foreheads to symbolize how the filters affect incoming sensory information. Then suggest various simple situations and ask participants to interpret what they see in the situations through the core beliefs on their coffee filters. The situations can be things such as

- A Caucasian man stumbles on the sidewalk in front of you and scrapes his knee.
- Your boss tells you that you made a mistake on an order you filled earlier in the day.
- Someone whispers something to you in a large group session and when you answer him, you're pulled up for disrupting the group.
- A man you know slightly asks you to do him a big favor and deliver a package to a neighbor of yours, but he doesn't bother to tell you what's in the package.
- A store clerk who is an African American woman asks to see your ID for a credit card or check purchase.
- You are called into an office for a job interview and when you step through the door, you realize for the first time that the person interviewing you is a woman.
- Your therapist says he or she needs to see you in his or her office after group.

Almost any situation will do. As you tell the participants the situation, ask them to imagine that what they see, hear, or sense about the situation—the information they are taking in—is passing through all their core belief filters before reaching their brain. Ask each participant to give you two or three thoughts that he might have in that situation as a result of his assigned core belief filters. Discuss the responses with the group. Are they realistically related to the core beliefs? How did the core beliefs "color" the thoughts they might have in response to the situation?

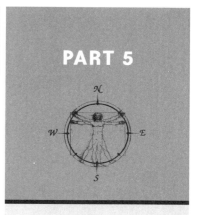
Criminality and Addiction on a Continuum

To review, there are four aspects of your criminal and addictive thinking. They are

1. thinking distortions
2. criminal thinking patterns
3. addictive thinking patterns
4. core beliefs

Facilitator Note

The ideas in this section may be best presented in lecture format rather than as a reading assignment, particularly if the participants in your group read at a low reading level or have learning disabilities. Presenting the ideas first in lecture format and then as a reading assignment is optimal.

Now that you are beginning to understand your criminal and addictive thinking and how that thinking has gotten you into trouble, it's time to look at the big picture. Looking at the big picture will help you better see

1. where you are now

2. how you got here

3. where you're headed if you don't change your thinking

4. where you could go if you *do* change your thinking

The big picture is called the continuum of criminality and the continuum of addiction. As you learned earlier, a *continuum* is a line that represents movement from one place to another (and sometimes back again).

As both a criminal and an addict, you are living your life on both the continuum of criminality *and* the continuum of addiction. While you may move back and forth a little bit, for the most part you have been moving in just one direction—getting worse.

The Continuum of Criminality

The four "stops" or stages on the continuum of criminality are the following:

- being responsible
- being irresponsible (noncriminal)
- being irresponsible (criminal)
- being an extreme criminal

Figure 17
THE CONTINUUM OF CRIMINALITY

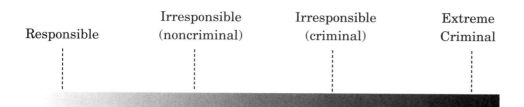

Responsible   Irresponsible (noncriminal)   Irresponsible (criminal)   Extreme Criminal

Each of these stages is identified by certain behavior and thinking tendencies. Here are the tendencies:

Responsible

____ Has a pattern of accepting responsibility at home, at work, and in society

____ Has a lifestyle based on hard work and fulfilling obligations

____ Has consideration of others

____ Gets self-respect and the respect of others through achievement

____ Desires to violate may happen, but they disappear without having to make a conscious choice

____ Does not violate the rights or property of others

____ Makes choices that are in the best interests of both self and others

____ Trusts the judgment of others

Irresponsible (noncriminal)

____ Accepts only a small amount of responsibility and makes excuses

____ Willing to lie, manipulate, and intimidate to get his way

____ Generally unreliable and chronically late—may perform poorly at work

____ Often fails to carry out promises and obligations at home

Facilitator Note
Participants may be tempted to start checking items on these lists. Encourage them to wait until they reach exercise 75 and then follow the directions given there.

____ Expects to fail and makes only halfhearted attempts

____ Lacks goal-oriented direction

Irresponsible (criminal)

____ Accepts responsibility only when backed into a corner but then fights it all the way

____ Has the thinking patterns of the extreme criminal but with less extensive crime patterns

____ Is a minor violator who rarely gets caught

____ Is very secretive and isolated from others

____ Feels successful because he hasn't been caught for much of his criminal activity

____ Has desires to violate but doesn't most of the time

____ Without restraints, will commit violations previously only thought about

____ Moves away from family or to different city or area to decrease restraints (be more free to offend) and to be more unknown (incognito)

Extreme Criminal

____ Accepts little or no responsibility

____ Has a continuous flow of criminal thoughts

____ Has concern only for self—defends self at all costs

____ Sees self as a good person, not a criminal

____ Seeks to promote self at the expense of others

____ Exploits relationships for self-profit

____ Criticizes others, blames others, and claims injustice when things don't go his way

____ Sees being nice as a weakness

____ Is overconfident and grandiose—won't stop trying to beat the system

Where Are You on the Continuum of Criminality?

➤ Review the four "stops" on the continuum of criminality. Place an X beside the items that apply to you. Think about what led up to the offense that brought you behind bars the last time. *Be honest with yourself.* Learning to tell yourself the truth about yourself is the first step in your recovery from both addiction and criminality.

➤ Looking back, where do you think you were on the continuum of criminality when you were incarcerated this last time?

_____

➤ Why do you think that? Which characteristics of that "stop" on the continuum describe you especially well?

_____

_____

_____

➤ Do you think you are still in the same "stop" on the continuum of criminality as you were when you were locked up this most recent time? Why or why not?

_____

_____

_____

Facilitator Note

The intent here is to see if the participant claims progress with his addiction and criminality since he has been incarcerated. If so, his answer to the last part of this exercise will be different from his answer to the first part. If the participant does claim significant progress, it could be a variation of his criminal pride or an effort at false compliance. Although it is unlikely that he has been spending his time behind bars engaged in sincere soul-searching, it is possible. You may want to challenge the answers and go deeper if you believe this is the case.

The Life Course of the Criminal-Addict and the Noncriminal-Nonaddict

How did you happen to become a criminal-addict? Figure 18a shows the life course of the noncriminal-nonaddict and Figure 18b shows the life course of the criminal-addict.

Figure 18a
THE NONCRIMINAL-NONADDICT LIFE COURSE

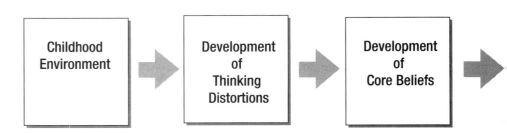

Figure 18b
THE CRIMINAL-ADDICT LIFE COURSE

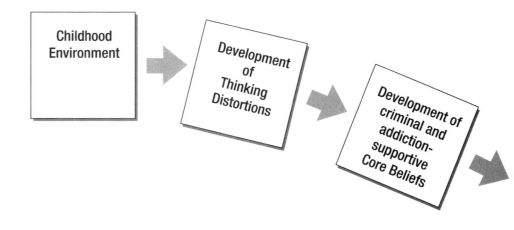

As you can see, everyone comes from a childhood environment that includes family, community, and physical and material conditions. For some people, those conditions are nurturing, safe, and bountiful. For others they are cruel, dangerous, and deprived. Most people's childhood environments fall somewhere in between those two extremes.

You may think that you're a criminal and addict because your childhood was particularly hard. Growing up in a cruel, dangerous, or deprived environment may

Development of noncriminal and nonaddict thinking patterns → The noncriminal/nonaddict life course

contribute toward the decision to take a criminal life path or turn to chemicals. Resentments, anger at the unfairness of life, and fear for survival poison the mind and can direct a person toward disconnecting from society. But that disconnection is also a *choice. And it is a choice you made.*

Not everybody made that choice. As you learned in exercise 22 on page 95, not everyone who grew up where you did and experienced what you did became a criminal or an addict. Most, in fact, did not—because they *chose* not to.

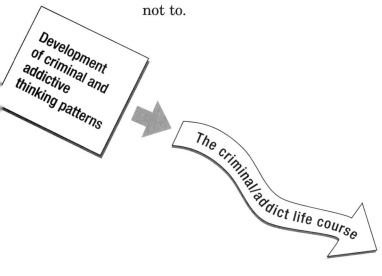

Development of criminal and addictive thinking patterns → The criminal/addict life course

Why did you choose crime and drugs? Because you developed core beliefs that supported criminal and addictive thinking patterns. It is your criminal and addictive thinking patterns that sent you on the downward slide into criminality and addiction.

After all, there are problems, and there is how you *handle* problems. The choices you make about how to handle your problems can be either criminal or noncriminal; courageous and straightforward or an escape into drugs or alcohol.

Understanding what happened when you left the non-criminal-nonaddict life will help you better understand how to stop the downward slide and begin to move back up into recovery and responsible living.

The Progression of Criminal Development

The continuum of criminality helps show you where you are in your criminal life. It helps describe you as you are. It does not show you how you got there or where you're headed. The steps you took into a criminal life can also be seen in stages. Your movement into the criminal life is a downward slide or progression. Again, there are four stages of this progression. Each has identifying characteristics, behaviors, and ways of thinking.

The progression of criminal development is shown on the next page. You can see that the five stages of criminal development are

1. pre-criminal stage

2. early criminal stage

3. middle criminal stage

4. late criminal stage

5. denial stage

Figure 19
THE PROGRESSION OF CRIMINAL DEVELOPMENT

Pre-Criminal Stage

___ Arrests for nuisance and status-type offenses (show-off, to get a "rep")

___ Vandalism, larceny, burglary, and auto theft are popular crimes

___ Crimes are committed in the company of groups or gangs

___ Peer pressure is an important influence in the decision to offend

___ Crimes are committed for excitement (though less severe crimes than in later stages)

___ The best chance to change happens here (about half in this stage drop out of the criminal life)

Early Criminal Stage

___ Greater investment of time, energy, and interest in crime

___ Thrills, status, and peer acceptance are no longer important reasons for committing crimes

___ Contemplate crime as a career or lifestyle

___ Frequency of crime drops, but the severity increases; the desire for power and control over others, greed, and an "I don't care" attitude increase

___ Desire for money to get drugs and nonessential material things increases

Middle Criminal Stage

___ Committed to a criminal way of life

___ Anger and resentment become primary motivations for crime

___ Increasing concern with power and control over others

___ Lowest frequency and highest severity of crime

___ Count on the "Big Score" to make everything all right

___ Criminal lifestyle frenzy is very dangerous to self and others—greater and more risks are taken

Late Criminal Stage

___ Decreased physical strength, stamina, and activity

___ Less concern with material things and awareness of crime as a "no-win" way of life

___ Fear of growing old and dying behind bars

___ Burnout: wearing down due to age and the accumulation of negative consequences

___ Maturity: re-evaluation of life goals and priorities (while burnout is expected, maturity may or may not happen)

Denial Stage

This is a "bottoming out" or pre-recovery stage. Denial is part of every stage in the entire downward progression of criminality and addiction, but it is also the state in which recovery must begin.

___ Still doesn't recognize a problem and is resistant to change—is in full denial

___ Continues to minimize behavior by comparing self to others who are worse or behaviors that are worse

___ Still rationalizes behavior by putting a positive spin on it, dismissing it as history, or portraying self as the victim

It's a steep slope from the pre-criminal stage to the late criminal stage. You start at the top and it carries you swiftly to the bottom. Recovery can begin at any stage in the process. You don't have to hit rock-bottom first. Breaking through the denial prevents you from reaching or staying at the bottom.

Here are the characteristics that define each stage:

Pre-Criminal Stage

____ Arrests for nuisance and status-type offenses (show-off, to get a "rep")

____ Vandalism, larceny, burglary, and auto theft are popular crimes

____ Crimes are committed in the company of groups or gangs

____ Peer pressure is an important influence in the decision to offend

____ Crimes are committed for excitement (though less severe crimes than in later stages)

____ The best chance to change happens here (about half in this stage drop out of the criminal life)

Early Criminal Stage

____ Greater investment of time, energy, and interest in crime

____ Thrills, status, and peer acceptance are no longer important reasons for committing crimes

____ Contemplate crime as a career or lifestyle

____ Frequency of crimes drop, but the severity increases; the desire for power and control over others, greed, and "I don't care" attitude increase

____ Desire for money to get drugs and nonessential material things increases

Facilitator Note

Participants may be tempted to start checking items on these lists. Encourage them to wait until they reach exercise 76 and then follow the directions given there.

Middle Criminal Stage

____ Committed to a criminal way of life

____ Anger and resentment become primary motivations for crime

____ Increasing concern with power and control over others

____ Lowest frequency and highest severity of crime

____ Count on the "Big Score" to make everything all right

____ Criminal lifestyle frenzy is very dangerous to self and others—greater and more risks are taken

Late Criminal Stage

____ Decreased physical strength, stamina, and activity

____ Less concern with material things and awareness of crime as a "no-win" way of life

____ Fear of growing old and dying behind bars.

____ Burnout: wearing down due to age and the accumulation of negative consequences

____ Maturity: re-evaluation of life goals and priorities (While burnout is expected, maturity may or may not happen.)

Denial Stage

This is a "bottoming out" or prerecovery stage. Denial is part of every stage in the entire downward progression of criminality and addiction, but it is also the state in which recovery must begin.

____ Still doesn't recognize a problem and is resistant to change—is in full denial

____ Continues to minimize behavior by comparing self to others who are worse or behaviors that are worse

____ Still rationalizes behavior by putting a positive spin on it, dismissing it as history, or portraying self as the victim

Facilitator Note
Denial may come in two forms. One is a psychological condition in which the person truly does not see the irrationality of his thinking. Offenders, however, may have a tendency to use denial more as an excuse or tactic to rationalize continuing with old behaviors. Phrases such as "I only did [this type of crime]," "That's not me," "I'd never do that," or "That may apply to others here, but not me," show a manipulative version of denial common with criminal offenders. It is possible to have both types of denial at the same time. This complicates your efforts to determine where the participant is in his treatment process. Keep in mind that each participant must be challenged differently.

What Stage of Your
Criminal Development Are You In?

➤ You've already identified where you think you are on the criminal continuum. The progression of criminal development tells you a little bit more about how you moved into your criminal career. Reread the characteristics of the five stages on pages 238–239 and put an **X** by the ones that apply to you.

➤ Judging from the characteristics that you checked, what stage in the development of your criminal career were you in when you were locked up this last time?

_____

_____

➤ Why do you think that? Which characteristics in that stage most describe your criminal life?

_____

_____

_____

_____

_____

_____

Look again at figure 19. Notice the circle at the bottom of the line that is moving downward into criminality from left to right.

That circle represents the opportunity for change.

It's the chance you have right now to turn your life around and start back up again. No matter what stage you are at in the progression of your criminal development, you can place that circle right where you are now and begin the climb toward responsible living.

The Progression of Criminal Recovery

Just as there are stages in the progression of criminal development, there are also stages in criminal recovery. You can see by looking at figure 20 (on the next page) that it doesn't happen overnight. It will take time and effort to move through the stages toward building a life that won't bring you back to where you are right now. But it can be done. The stages of criminal recovery show you the path.

Figure 20 shows the five stages in the progression of criminal recovery. They are

1. bargaining stage
2. early recovery stage
3. middle recovery stage
4. late recovery stage
5. maintenance stage

You can begin the climb toward responsible living.

Figure 20
THE PROGRESSION OF RECOVERY

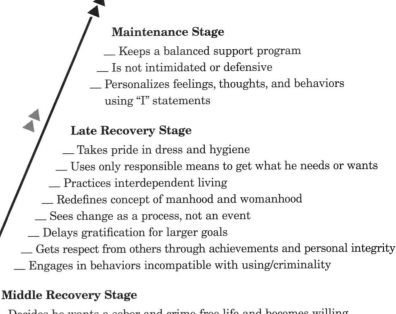

The goal of the progression of recovery is to move on up the slope. You begin at the bottom—the bargaining stage. Here, the decision to change is made.

Maintenance Stage

__ Keeps a balanced support program

__ Is not intimidated or defensive

__ Personalizes feelings, thoughts, and behaviors using "I" statements

Late Recovery Stage

__ Takes pride in dress and hygiene

__ Uses only responsible means to get what he needs or wants

__ Practices interdependent living

__ Redefines concept of manhood and womanhood

__ Sees change as a process, not an event

__ Delays gratification for larger goals

__ Gets respect from others through achievements and personal integrity

__ Engages in behaviors incompatible with using/criminality

Middle Recovery Stage

__ Decides he wants a sober and crime-free life and becomes willing to do whatever it takes

__ No longer sees self as victim

__ Becomes increasingly honest with self and others

__ Recognizes obligations and makes genuine effort to fulfill promises most of the time

__ Admits wrong when makes a mistake and tries to make amends most of the time

__ Makes rational decisions based on fact most of the time

__ Finds merit in being competent in a job

__ Deemphasizes power struggles and doesn't seek control; considers others and seeks solutions that can benefit all most of the time

Early Recovery Stage

__ Intention to change plus *some* effort to do so

__ Asks questions, though usually the wrong questions, such as, "Why is the world out to get me?"

__ Seeks to control anger, criminal impulse, and impulse to use alcohol or drugs by force of will

__ Does the minimum to get by (false compliance) rather than fully committing to a sober, crime-free lifestyle

__ May not see need for more effective action and get stuck at this stage

__ May begin to understand that recovery involves daily choices that support not using and not committing crimes

Bargaining Stage

This is a pre-recovery stage. Bargaining may be part of the downward progression of criminality and addiction, but it is also the beginning of an awareness that change is needed.

__ General awareness of a problem but not sure what it is

__ Still tends to project the problem onto other people or external circumstances

__ Thinks about need for change, but only "sometime in the future"

__ Has a magical or wishful view of change—that it will just happen without personal effort

__ Thinks more about what is comfortable than what needs to be done

__ Makes external changes such as the "geographical cure" (moving to a new place to escape past behaviors) in mistaken belief it will fix everything

__ Makes deals, such as only weekend use or only property crime or will sell but not use

Here are the characteristics that define these stages:

Bargaining Stage

This is a pre-recovery stage. Bargaining may be part of the downward progression of criminality and addiction, but it is also the beginning of an awareness that change is needed.

____ General awareness of a problem but not sure what it is

____ Still tends to project the problem onto other people or external circumstances

____ Thinks about need for change, but only "sometime in the future"

____ Has a magical or wishful view of change—that it will just happen without personal effort

____ Thinks more about what is comfortable than what needs to be done

____ Makes external changes such as the "geographical cure" (moving to a new place to escape past behaviors) in mistaken belief it will fix everything

____ Makes deals, such as only weekend use or only property crime or will sell but not use

Early Recovery Stage

____ Intention to change plus *some* effort to do so

____ Asks questions, though usually the wrong questions, such as, "Why is the world out to get me?"

____ Seeks to control anger, criminal impulse, and the impulse to use alcohol or drugs by force of will

____ Does the minimum to get by (false compliance) rather than fully committing to a sober, crime-free lifestyle

____ May not see need for more effective action and get stuck at this stage

____ May begin to understand that recovery involves daily choices that support not using and not committing crimes

Middle Recovery Stage

____ Decides he wants a sober and crime-free life and becomes willing to do whatever it takes

____ No longer sees self as victim

____ Becomes increasingly honest with self and others.

____ Recognizes obligations and makes genuine effort to fulfill promises most of the time

____ Admits wrong when makes a mistake and tries to make amends most of the time

____ Makes rational decisions based on fact most of the time

____ Finds merit in being competent in a job

____ Deemphasizes power struggles and doesn't seek control; considers others and seeks solutions that can benefit all most of the time

Late Recovery Stage

____ Takes pride in dress and hygiene

____ Uses only responsible means to get what he needs or wants

____ Practices interdependent living

____ Redefines concept of manhood and womanhood

____ Sees change as a process, not an event

____ Delays gratification for larger goals

____ Gets respect from others through achievements and personal integrity

____ Engages in behaviors incompatible with using or criminality

Maintenance Stage

____ Keeps a balanced support program

____ Is not intimidated or defensive

____ Personalizes feelings, thoughts, and behaviors using
"I" statements

The time and effort your recovery from criminality takes
depends on the following:

1. where you are in your progression of criminal
   development (the downward slide)

2. how committed you are to turning the course of
   your life around

3. other factors

There will be setbacks; there will be frustrations. How
difficult your recovery will be also depends on how well
you deal with these setbacks and frustrations.

Figure 21
THE PROGRESSION OF CRIMINAL DEVELOPMENT AND RECOVERY

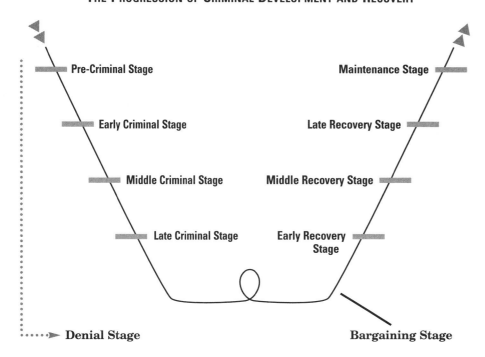

Pre-Criminal Stage

Early Criminal Stage

Middle Criminal Stage

Late Criminal Stage

Maintenance Stage

Late Recovery Stage

Middle Recovery Stage

Early Recovery Stage

Denial Stage

Bargaining Stage

Have You Made the Decision to Recover from Criminality?

Remember, the circle at the bottom of figure 21 represents the decision to turn your life around, to seek recovery. Think about whether you have really made that decision.

➤ Place an **X** next to the statement that is most true for you.

_____ **Yes,** I have made the decision to turn my life around.

_____ **No,** I have not yet committed to leaving the criminal life.

➤ If you chose yes, what choices will you make to turn your life around?

_____

_____

_____

➤ If you chose no, what will it take for you to make that decision? Why don't you want to give up the criminal life?

_____

_____

_____

_____

What Stage of Your Criminal Recovery Are You In?

➤ What stage of your recovery from criminality are you in?

_____

_____

_____

➤ Why do you think you are in that stage?

_____

_____

_____

➤ How does your thinking and behavior reflect this?

_____

_____

_____

Facilitator Note
Some participants might not be able to see themselves on the progression of recovery. After all, many offenders are fatalistic about the possibility of change and growth. If necessary, have peers complete this assignment for the doubtful participant. This will show the participant that he _has_ made some steps, however tentative, toward a better life.

The Continuum of Addiction

Just as there is a continuum of criminality, there is also a continuum of addiction. It also has four "stops" or stages. They are

- responsible use
- irresponsible use
- abuse/early addiction
- advanced addiction

Figure 22
THE CONTINUUM OF ADDICTION

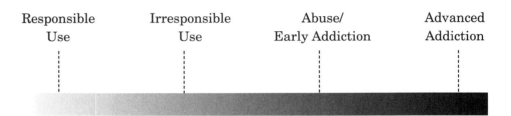

| Responsible Use | Irresponsible Use | Abuse/ Early Addiction | Advanced Addiction |

Each of these "stops" on the continuum has certain features:

Responsible Use

____ Occasional alcohol use in social settings

____ Does not drink to get drunk

____ Does not violate the law to use (does not use illegal substances)

____ Does not drive after drinking

____ Does not go out of way to get a drink

____ Does not lie and is not secretive about drinking

Irresponsible Use

____ Occasionally drinks to excess

____ Uses illegal substances to get high once in a while

____ Sometimes drives after using

Facilitator Note

It is important to emphasize that occasional, limited alcohol use is only responsible use for nonaddicts.

For addicts and alcoholics, **any** alcohol use is irresponsible. Any **illegal** drug use is always irresponsible for everybody.

Facilitator Note

Participants may be tempted to start checking items on these lists. Encourage them to wait until they reach exercise 79 and then follow the directions given there.

____ Sometimes uses to feel better, to relieve stress, or to alter unhappy or sad feelings

____ Provides illegal substances to others or alcohol to minors to have company in using

____ Underage drinking

Abuse/Early Addiction

____ Regularly uses to get drunk or high, even before work or family events

____ Uses almost every time when feels bad

____ Sometimes violates own morals and values in order to use or when using

____ Associates almost entirely with irresponsible users, abusers, and addicts

____ Makes excuses and lies about using

____ Has frequent problems with family and work because of using

____ Creates rituals around using and buys many products associated with using

____ Neglects healthy diet and develops irregular sleep patterns

____ Tries the "geographical cure," moves away in attempt to start over

Advanced Addiction

____ Has powerful cravings for drugs or alcohol and a need to relieve them

____ Has unpleasant withdrawal symptoms (with alcohol and most—but not all—other drugs) if can't get supply or tries to stop

____ Life revolves entirely around using (loss of other interests)

____ Isolates self from most or all friends and family members

____ Violates own morals and values regularly in order to use

____ Is full of undefined fears; has irrational suspicions of others

EXERCISE 79 EXERCISE

Where Are You on the Continuum of Addiction?

Facilitator Note

Encourage the participants to answer this honestly. Point out that they are incarcerated, so they might be further down the continuum than they'd like to admit.

Review the four "stops" on the continuum of addiction on pages 248–250. Place a mark beside the ones that apply to you, especially to your life before you were incarcerated this last time.

➤ Where do you think you were on the continuum of addiction when you were incarcerated this last time?

_____

_____

_____

➤ Why do you think that? Which characteristics of that "stop" on the continuum describe you especially well?

_____

_____

_____

The Progression of Addiction

The continuum of addiction helps you see where you are in your addiction, but it doesn't show how you got there. Just as there was a progression of stages that you followed into criminality, there is also a progression of stages into addiction. These stages are:

1. use
2. early stage
3. middle stage (crucial phase)
4. late stage (chronic phase)
5. denial stage

These stages also come with identifying characteristics, behaviors, and ways of thinking. The progression of addiction development is shown on the next page.

As figure 23 on page 252 shows, here are the characteristics that define each stage:

Use

____ Experimentation

____ Uses in the company of peers

____ Moderate or occasional use

____ Social or recreational use

____ Moderate and frequent use

____ Moderate but habitual use

____ Occasional use for "kicks" or "thrills"

Early Stage

____ Pattern of amount and frequency of use which, if continued, has high potential of leading to abuse and addiction

____ Uses to relieve stress, to make self feel better

Facilitator Note
Participants may be tempted to start checking items below. Encourage them to wait until they reach exercise 80 and then follow the directions given there.

Figure 23
THE PROGRESSION OF ADDICTION DEVELOPMENT

Use
— Experimentation
— Uses in the company of peers
— Moderate or occasional use
— Social or recreational use
— Moderate and frequent use
— Moderate but habitual use
— Occasional use for "kicks" or "thrills"

Early Stage
— Pattern of amount and frequency of use which, if continued, has high potential of leading to abuse and addiction
— Uses to relieve stress, to make self feel better
— Frequent use for "kicks" or "thrills"
— Uses with intent to get high or drunk
— Spree use (heavy use over more than one day)
— Occasional use of excessive amounts to extreme intoxication

Middle Stage (Crucial Phase)
— Amount and frequency of use interferes with "normal" functioning in society
— Regular spree use, use for "thrills," and intent to get high or drunk
— Increasing use of excessive amounts to extreme intoxication
— Habitual use of excessive amounts to extreme intoxication
— Continued use despite experiencing negative reactions and consequences
— Lack of awareness of the degree of impairment while under the influence
— Plans to change use patterns but is easily drawn into old patterns
— Increase in tolerance—takes greater amount of the drug to achieve the high

Late Stage (Chronic Phase)
— Tries to stop using but can't
— Uses alone and hides use
— Continues to use despite harmful consequences
— Preoccupation, or obsession, with the drug
— Serious deterioration of physical and mental health
— Decrease in tolerance—lesser amount of the drug causes greater loss of control (with alcohol and some other drugs)
— Loses control of most aspects of life
— Bottoms out with loss of ability to function in the world

Denial Stage

This is a "bottoming out" or pre-recovery stage. Denial is part of every stage in the entire downward progression of criminality and addiction, but it is also the state in which recovery must begin.

— Still doesn't recognize a problem and is resistant to change—is in full denial

— Continues to minimize behavior by comparing self to others who are worse or behaviors that are worse

— Still rationalizes behavior by putting a positive spin on it, dismissing it as history, or portraying self as the victim

It's a steep slope from the beginning stage of addiction to the late stage. You start at the top and it carries you swiftly to the bottom. Recovery can begin at any stage in the process. You don't have to hit rock-bottom first. Breaking through the denial prevents you from reaching or staying at the bottom.

____ Frequent use for "kicks" or "thrills"

____ Uses with intent to get high or drunk

____ Spree use (heavy use over more than one day)

____ Occasional use of excessive amounts to extreme intoxication

Middle Stage (Crucial Phase)

____ Amount and frequency of use interferes with "normal" functioning in society

____ Regular spree use, use for "thrills," and intent to get high or drunk

____ Increasing use of excessive amounts to extreme intoxication

____ Habitual use of excessive amounts to extreme intoxication

____ Continued use despite experiencing negative reactions and consequences

____ Lack of awareness of the degree of impairment while under the influence

____ Plans to change use patterns but is easily drawn into old patterns

____ Increase in tolerance—takes greater amount of the drug to achieve the high

Late Stage (Chronic Phase)

____ Tries to stop using but can't

____ Uses alone and hides use

____ Continues to use despite harmful consequences

____ Preoccupation, or obsession, with the drug

____ Serious deterioration of physical and mental health

_____ Decrease in tolerance—lesser amount of the drug causes greater loss of control (with alcohol and some other drugs)

_____ Loses control of most aspects of life

_____ Bottoms out with loss of ability to function in the world

Denial Stage

This is a "bottoming out" or pre-recovery stage. Denial is part of every stage in the entire downward progression of criminality and addiction, but it is also the state in which recovery must begin.

_____ Still doesn't recognize a problem and is resistant to change—is in full denial

_____ Continues to minimize behavior by comparing self to others who are worse or behaviors that are worse

_____ Still rationalizes behavior by putting a positive spin on it, dismissing it as history, or portraying self as the victim

What Stage of Your Addiction Development Are You In?

➤ You've already identified where you think you are on the addiction continuum. The progression of addiction development tells you a little bit more about *how* you moved into your habitual chemical use. Review the characteristics of the five stages on pages 251 and 253–254 and put an **X** by the ones that apply to you.

➤ Judging from the characteristics that you marked, what stage in the development of your addiction were you in when you were locked up this last time?

_____

➤ Why do you think that? Which characteristics in that stage most describe how you used chemicals before you were locked up this most recent time?

_____

_____

_____

_____

Facilitator Note
After participants have completed exercise 80, you may choose to have a group discussion.

The Progression of Addiction Recovery

If you look again at figure 23, the progression of addiction development, you see that it also has a circle. As with the progression of criminal development, the circle represents the possibility—and opportunity—of changing the downward direction of your progression into addiction and moving back upward into recovery. And again, no matter where you are on the progression of addiction, your decision to seek recovery creates the circle and changes your direction.

Figure 24 on the following page shows the five stages in the progression of addiction recovery. They are

1. bargaining stage

2. early recovery stage

3. middle recovery stage

4. late recovery stage

5. maintenance stage

Here are the characteristics that define these stages:

Bargaining Stage

This is a pre-recovery stage. Bargaining may be part of the downward progression of criminality and addiction, but it is also the beginning of an awareness that change is needed.

____ General awareness of a problem but not sure what it is

____ Still tends to project the problem onto other people or external circumstances

____ Thinks about need for change, but only "sometime in the future"

____ Has a magical or wishful view of change—that it will just happen without personal effort

Figure 24
THE PROGRESSION OF RECOVERY

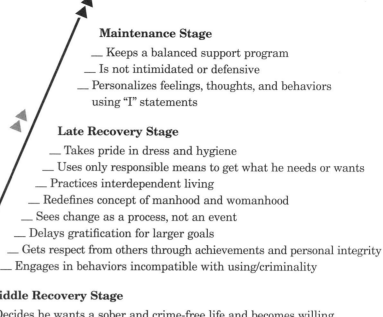

The goal of the progression of recovery is to move on up the slope. You begin at the bottom—the bargaining stage. Here, the decision to change is made.

Maintenance Stage
__ Keeps a balanced support program
__ Is not intimidated or defensive
__ Personalizes feelings, thoughts, and behaviors using "I" statements

Late Recovery Stage
__ Takes pride in dress and hygiene
__ Uses only responsible means to get what he needs or wants
__ Practices interdependent living
__ Redefines concept of manhood and womanhood
__ Sees change as a process, not an event
__ Delays gratification for larger goals
__ Gets respect from others through achievements and personal integrity
__ Engages in behaviors incompatible with using/criminality

Middle Recovery Stage
__ Decides he wants a sober and crime-free life and becomes willing to do whatever it takes
__ No longer sees self as victim
__ Becomes increasingly honest with self and others
__ Recognizes obligations and makes genuine effort to fulfill promises most of the time
__ Admits wrong when makes a mistake and tries to make amends most of the time
__ Makes rational decisions based on fact most of the time
__ Finds merit in being competent in a job
__ De-emphasizes power struggles and doesn't seek control. Considers others and seeks solutions that can benefit all most of the time

Early Recovery Stage
__ Intention to change plus *some* effort to do so
__ Asks questions, though usually the wrong questions, such as, "Why is the world out to get me?"
__ Seeks to control anger, criminal impulse, and impulse to use alcohol or drugs by force of will
__ Often does the minimum to get by (false compliance) rather than fully committing to a sober and crime-free lifestyle
__ May not see need for more effective action and may get stuck at this stage
__ May begin to understand that recovery involves daily choices that support not using and not committing crimes

Bargaining Stage
This is a pre-recovery stage. Bargaining may be part of the downward progression of criminality and addiction, but it is also the beginning of an awareness that change is needed.
__ General awareness of a problem but not sure what it is
__ Still tends to project the problem onto other people or external circumstances
__ Thinks about need for change, but only "sometime in the future"
__ Has a magical or wishful view of change—that it will just happen without personal effort
__ Thinks more about what is comfortable than what needs to be done
__ Makes external changes such as the "geographical cure" (moving to a new place to escape past behaviors) in mistaken belief it will fix everything
__ Makes deals, such as only weekend use or only property crime or will sell but not use

____ Thinks more about what is comfortable than what needs to be done

____ Makes external changes such as the "geographical cure" (moving to a new place to escape past behaviors) in mistaken belief it will fix everything

____ Makes deals, such as only weekend use or only property crime or will sell but not use

Early Recovery Stage

____ Intention to change plus *some* effort to do so

____ Asks questions, though usually the wrong questions, such as, "Why is the world out to get me?"

____ Seeks to control anger, criminal impulse, and the impulse to use alcohol or drugs by force of will

____ Often does the minimum to get by (false compliance) rather than fully committing to a sober and crime-free lifestyle

____ May not see need for more effective action and may get stuck at this stage

____ May begin to understand that recovery involves daily choices that support not using and not committing crimes

Middle Recovery Stage

____ Decides he wants a sober and crime-free life and becomes willing to do whatever it takes

____ No longer sees self as victim

____ Becomes increasingly honest with self and others

____ Recognizes obligations and makes genuine effort to fulfill promises most of the time

____ Admits wrong when makes a mistake and tries to make amends most of the time

____ Makes rational decisions based on fact most of the time

____ Finds merit in being competent in a job

____ De-emphasizes power struggles and doesn't seek control. Considers others and seeks solutions that can benefit all most of the time

Late Recovery Stage

____ Takes pride in dress and hygiene

____ Uses only responsible means to get what he needs or wants

____ Practices interdependent living

____ Redefines concept of manhood and womanhood

____ Sees change as a process, not an event

____ Delays gratification for larger goals

____ Gets respect from others through achievements and personal integrity

____ Engages in behaviors incompatible with using or criminality

Maintenance Stage

____ Keeps a balanced support program

____ Is not intimidated or defensive

____ Personalizes feelings, thoughts, and behaviors using "I" statements

As figure 24 on page 257 shows, recovery from addiction, like recovery from criminality, is also a progression. Over time, you will build a path to sobriety brick by brick, moving through the various stages toward reaching your life potential.

And again, the progression of recovery from addiction begins with the circle at the bottom, the decision to turn your life around and try something new: recovery.

Figure 25
THE PROGRESSION OF ADDICTION DEVELOPMENT AND RECOVERY

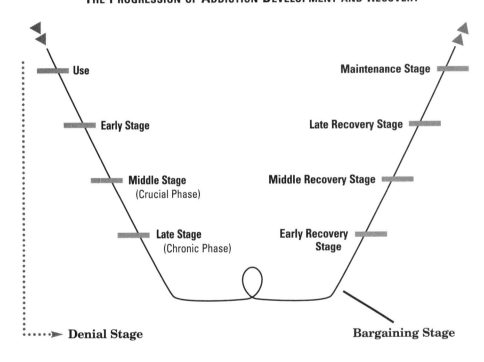

Use

Early Stage

Middle Stage
(Crucial Phase)

Late Stage
(Chronic Phase)

Denial Stage

Maintenance Stage

Late Recovery Stage

Middle Recovery Stage

Early Recovery
Stage

Bargaining Stage

No matter where you are on the progression of addiction, your decision to seek recovery creates the circle and changes your direction.

Have You Made the Decision to Recover from Addiction?

Remember, the circle at the bottom of figure 25 represents the decision to turn your life around, to seek recovery. Think about whether you have really made that decision.

➤ Place an **X** next to the statement that is most true for you.

＿＿＿ **Yes,** I have made the decision to turn my life around.

＿＿＿ **No,** I have not yet committed to leaving the using life.

➤ If you chose yes, what choices will you make to turn your life around?

＿＿＿＿＿＿＿＿＿＿＿＿＿＿＿＿＿＿＿＿＿＿＿＿＿＿＿＿＿

＿＿＿＿＿＿＿＿＿＿＿＿＿＿＿＿＿＿＿＿＿＿＿＿＿＿＿＿＿

＿＿＿＿＿＿＿＿＿＿＿＿＿＿＿＿＿＿＿＿＿＿＿＿＿＿＿＿＿

➤ If you chose no, what will it take for you to make that decision? Why don't you want to give up the using life?

＿＿＿＿＿＿＿＿＿＿＿＿＿＿＿＿＿＿＿＿＿＿＿＿＿＿＿＿＿

＿＿＿＿＿＿＿＿＿＿＿＿＿＿＿＿＿＿＿＿＿＿＿＿＿＿＿＿＿

＿＿＿＿＿＿＿＿＿＿＿＿＿＿＿＿＿＿＿＿＿＿＿＿＿＿＿＿＿

Facilitator Note

Participants need to realize how important this decision is. Without a desire to turn their lives around, recovery won't happen.

What Stage of Your Addiction Recovery Are You In?

➤ What stage of your recovery from addiction are you in? (If you don't think you've started yet, write "Haven't started.")

_____

_____

_____

➤ Why do you think you are in that stage?

_____

_____

_____

➤ How has your thinking and behavior shown this?

_____

_____

_____

Facilitator Note

Encourage the participants to answer exercise 82 honestly.

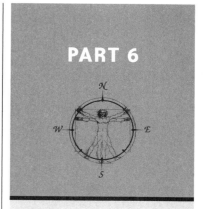

Learning to Think about Your Behavior

We've discussed thinking distortions, criminal and addictive thinking patterns, and core beliefs, and we've shown how all these can lead to irresponsible behavior. Remember, your *behavior* is the result of your *thinking*. Earlier in this workbook, you explored your habits of thinking. Now you'll look at some of your habits of behavior that resulted from that thinking.

Facilitator Note

Small-group discussion is particularly beneficial in this section on tactics. Participants will have a chance to come up with specific examples of how and why they have used the tactics (what they hoped to have happen). Discussion also allows them to explore whether criminal and addictive tactics, though helpful in getting them what they want in the short term, might sabotage their success in the long term.

Facilitator Note

The following pages may be best presented in lecture format rather than as a reading assignment, particularly if your group participants have a low reading level or learning disabilities. Presenting the ideas first in lecture form and then as a reading assignment is optimal.

Tactics

Tactics are planned behavior strategies and approaches intended to achieve a goal.

Behavior can be responsible, irresponsible (legal, but potentially damaging to you or others), or criminal (violating others in ways society prohibits by law). As we've seen with the continuum of criminality, a lot of irresponsible thinking and behavior and criminal thinking and behavior sit right next to each other—they're only slightly different. But since you are reading this in a treatment program behind bars, your thinking and behavior probably fits into either the "irresponsible and criminal" or "extreme criminal" stop on the continuum of criminality.

You have seriously broken the law at least once and perhaps many, many more times.

In fact, the odds are that you have done so much irresponsible behavior, both criminal and noncriminal, that you have developed patterns of behavior. These behavior strategies have worked well for you in manipulating, intimidating, controlling, and violating others. You have used these behaviors so often and so consistently that they have become habits for you. These habits of criminal and addictive behavior are called ***tactics.*** Because they are habits, you use these criminal and addictive tactics in almost everything you do. You are probably using them in this treatment program.

The use of criminal and addictive tactics is a habit of behavior you will have to change in order to recover from both your criminality and your alcohol and drug use. To change these habits and recover, you will need to understand the thinking behind the tactics—why you do what you do.

Criminal and Addictive Tactics

You use criminal and addictive tactics as a survival mechanism. You use them to avoid restrictions. You use them to get what you think you want. You use them to get people off your case or to avoid being held accountable for your behavior. And you also use them to avoid feeling put down or disrespected by others.

Who Uses Tactics?

Who uses tactics? Pretty much everybody. Generals, salespeople, parents, athletes, teachers, business managers, therapists, and others use tactics. Tactics are simply behaviors that are meant to get things done.

When responsible people use responsible tactics, they are intending to accomplish something helpful and worthwhile for themselves, their families, or their communities. The key is that they are not willing to use tactics in a way that violates the rights of others.

When irresponsible people use irresponsible tactics, they are trying to get something for themselves without earning it. They hide their true motives to take advantage of others and avoid responsibility.

When criminals use criminal tactics, they are trying to avoid being held accountable. They want to promote their criminal and addictive life—to get what they think they are entitled to or to avoid the feelings of zero state.

Avoiding and Escaping the Zero State

Remember the discussion of the criminal's and addict's zero state on pages 195–196? The biggest fear of all is falling into the zero state. You don't want to appear weak or indecisive or not in control. The zero state can result when others see your irresponsible thinking and behavior. It makes you feel worthless, empty, nothing—like you barely even exist.

Facilitator Note

You may choose to review the *Criminal & Addictive Behavior: Tactics* video at this time

Facilitator Note

It may be useful to gather several examples of criminal tactics used by participants in group over the past week and present them here. You can even put the participant's name to the example: "What is a criminal tactic? Well, when Mr. X claimed [this] a few days ago, what was he really trying to do? Was he trying to further his recovery or was he trying to [avoid effort/divert attention/aggressively attempt to keep the focus off himself]? Or how about when Mr. Y said . . .?" and so on. This shows dramatically how pervasive the use of criminal tactics is among participants.

You desperately try to avoid the zero state because you can't stand being in it. Criminal and addictive tactics help you avoid it. Once in the zero state, you desperately try to get out by using criminal and addictive tactics.

Fulfilling Your Sense of Entitlement

It is very important to remember that criminal and addictive tactics are not used just to escape or avoid the zero state. They are also used as the result of a powerful sense of entitlement—"I deserve to have whatever I want" or "I deserve to always feel good." Either way, tactics are a way to get what you want when you want it and to keep others from getting in your way.

How You Use Tactics

Criminal and addictive tactics are divided into these three types of strategies:

1. avoidance

2. diversion

3. aggression

You use *avoidance strategies* to escape responsibility, to keep a low profile so you won't have to put out effort or be exposed, and to manipulate others to get what you want.

You use *diversion strategies* to confuse others, to direct attention away from yourself or from the important issues, and to avoid exposure by keeping those around you distracted and focused on other things.

You use *aggression strategies* to attack, intimidate, and undermine the efforts of others. You actively try to create chaos by stirring up conflict, resentment, and other hard feelings.

You use avoidance strategies to escape responsibility.

The use of all three types of criminal and addictive tactics is the source of your feelings of criminal excitement and power. These strategies fuel your anger, resentment, and sense of entitlement. They help you deny the need for change by helping you deny your criminal and addictive thinking patterns, thinking distortions, and faulty core beliefs. They prevent you from setting goals for change.

Most criminals and addicts use all the tactics but in different orders. For example, you may prefer avoidance strategies, but if you run through all the avoidance tactics in a situation and they aren't working, you may flip over to diversion strategies. If those don't work, you'll try aggression strategies, and so on. Each person has his favorite tactics that he uses most often, but every criminal and addict is ready and willing to use any tactic that works in a situation.

For all these reasons, it is important that you understand one thing about your habits of behavior: *As a criminal and addictive thinker, you cannot make progress in treatment until you give up the excitement and power of using these criminal and addictive tactics and committing crimes or getting high.* And that has to start right now, in treatment. The first step in dealing with your use of criminal tactics is to name the tactics you use and learn to see them in your behavior. Then you can begin adding your tactics to your Thinking Reports.

Why is this just the first step? Because although understanding is crucial to change, it is not change. As your understanding of your use of tactics grows, you will begin the real work of recovery: letting go of old, irresponsible habits of living and substituting new, responsible ones *(new behaviors)* that will help you get along better in the world.

Avoidance Strategies

Here are the seven basic criminal and addictive tactics you use to get away with irresponsible thinking and behavior by avoidance:

1. lying by omission or commission (passive and active lying)

2. being deliberately vague

3. staying silent to avoid notice

4. false compliance
   a. compliance without commitment
   b. passive resistance compliance

5. playing dumb

6. selective memory and attention

7. minimizing (trivializing)

TACTIC 1:

Lying by Omission or Commission

Lying by omission or commission means misleading others by hiding the truth or telling half-truths (lying by omission, or passive lying) or misleading them by telling them things that are not true (lying by commission, or active lying). One is not better or worse than the other: A lie is a lie. You use lies to avoid getting caught, to hold power over others (withholding information can be powerful), to avoid accountability, and to continue your lifestyle.

You are lying by *omission* when you

- believe only you know what is important to disclose and what isn't

- disclose only the information that benefits you while withholding other important information, often by leaving out important details

- say "I don't know" or "I don't remember" when pressured for details; you do this as a way of avoiding accountability or an uncomfortable situation when in fact you *do* know

- use lead-in phrases like "to tell the truth" or "to be perfectly honest," usually a sure tip-off that you're withholding something

- twist facts and distort situations by shifting the emphasis onto minor facts while omitting crucial parts of the story

You are lying by *commission* when you

- make up stories to cover yourself and put others off the track

- deny to yourself or others what you know to be true

- believe that the truth works against your best interests and act accordingly

- distort, invent, turn upside down, or deny facts

TACTIC 2:

Being Deliberately Vague

Being deliberately vague means distorting the truth by fudging details, being intentionally uncertain of times and places, and trying to answer questions with wishy-washy generalities. Frequently claiming "I don't know" or "I can't remember" is one way of being deliberately vague. You use this tactic so you don't get pinned down. It's another way you avoid accountability and refuse to make a commitment to recovery. You think that vague statements will be enough to get people off your back without your having to confront your thinking and behavior and make changes. And you think that if others don't call you on it, then that's their problem. At least you didn't have to lie to them, and you can still tell yourself you're an honest person (even though you're not).

You are being deliberately vague when you

- talk and talk and talk about yourself without ever revealing any relevant information

- edit stories to give a false general impression that you were the victim instead of the victimizer

- try to conceal something by using words and phrases such as

  - "You might say . . ."

  - "Perhaps . . ."

  - "In a way . . ."

  - "Probably . . ."

  - "You could put it that way . . ."

  - "I suppose so . . ."

- avoid giving direct answers to direct questions

- use empty, nondisclosing phrases such as

  - "We talked about this and that . . ."

  - "You know what I'm saying . . ."

  - "If I feel like it . . ."

  - "It's going okay . . ."

  - "Someone told me . . ."

- say, "I'll think about it," when you're pinned down, though you never bring it up again. When you're challenged, you say, "I forgot"

Facilitator Note

Encourage participants to come up with examples of being deliberately vague. This might best be achieved during group session since this tactic is easily recognizable in others.

TACTIC 3:

Staying Silent to Avoid Notice

Staying silent to avoid notice could also be called "trying to fly under the radar." Again, you try to avoid being challenged by "blending into the woodwork." You hope that if you keep your mouth shut, everyone will ignore you and you can cruise through life—and your treatment program—without putting in any effort.

The purpose of silence is to maintain your criminal and addictive lifestyle through secrecy. It is also a way to control others and to keep others at a distance. Sometimes you use silence to buy yourself time to size up another person so you can figure out how to manipulate him or her.

You use silence as a criminal tactic when you

- say, "I don't know and I don't care"

- refuse to listen or participate

- say, "I have no comment on that"

- say, "I just can't explain it" while shrugging or sighing

- say, "Nothing happened"

- say, "I don't have anything to say. They said it all"

Facilitator Note

Encourage participants to come up with examples of staying silent to avoid notice. This might best be achieved during group session since this tactic is easily recognizable in others.

TACTIC 4:

False Compliance

Like lying, *false compliance* shows up in two ways: compliance without commitment and passive resistance.

In your treatment program, *compliance without commitment* is an attempt to con the therapists into thinking that you're doing the work and making changes, while in fact you're just saying what you think they want to hear so they won't challenge you. You say the "right" things to staff, but you don't really mean what you say. You think that if you can keep the therapists happy, they won't notice that you're really just putting in time. You've also probably used compliance without commitment with your family, your spouse or partner, and an employer to get them off your case.

Passive resistance is a type of false compliance where you do the absolute minimum to get by. Not one little bit more. You don't actively fight the system, but you're determined not to give in to it by looking at your thinking and behavior and making changes.

Again, false compliance is an effort to look like you're doing what you're supposed to be doing, while in reality you are not doing the work. You appear to be agreeable to change, but you are really undermining opportunities for real change. In other words, you "talk the talk," but you don't "walk the walk." In the program, you learn all the right words and phrases—treatment talk—and use them like they mean something to you. But they don't. It's just another tactic you use to keep the spotlight off of you and your criminal and addictive thinking patterns.

You are using false compliance as a criminal tactic when you

- try to "score points" by saying the right thing or by doing the right thing just one time

- tell different people different versions of your thoughts and experiences depending on what you think they want to hear or what will make you look good in their eyes

- promise to change by saying, "I'll never do it again"

- claim to have changed by doing something right once

- try to convince therapists that you've completed treatment and learned everything you need to stay sober and crime free when in fact you're just restless, bored, and seeking excitement

- claim to have had a miraculous transformation

- say yes without meaning it

- fake interest with intense concentration, eye contact, and nodding head

- say, "I guess so," "You're right," or "It makes sense to me," when in fact you don't agree or it doesn't make sense to you or you simply don't care

TACTIC 5:

Playing Dumb

Playing dumb is an act you put on to try to convince others that you are too fragile, helpless, or stupid to be responsible so that they'll let you off the hook. Or you may tell staff you'd really like to look at those issues if only you had an idea of what they are talking about. Again, you try to fool others into thinking you're just not capable of making a responsible effort or don't understand what it is they are asking you to look at. You use this tactic to escape having to work at change.

You use playing dumb as a criminal tactic when you

- pretend to have less education or a lower reading ability than you really have in order to get out of making an effort

- frequently complain, "I didn't understand the question" or "I don't know what you are talking about" without making an effort to understand

- look blankly when you are confronted or challenged, as if you're incapable of understanding the situation and giving a meaningful response

- make simplistic or off-base comments in order to appear lost and confused

- exaggerate or make up mental or physical health problems to excuse your lack of compliance or effort

- complain about having too much to do or that the work is too hard

Facilitator Note
Encourage participants to come up with examples of playing dumb. This might best be achieved during group session since this tactic is easily recognizable in others.

TACTIC 6:

Selective Memory and Attention

Selective memory and attention is yet another tactic for avoiding accountability. You remember only what's convenient to remember, so you won't be challenged or exposed. You also pay attention only to what you want to hear. You tune out anything that would make you uncomfortable about your criminal and addictive thinking and behavior.

You use selective memory and attention as a criminal tactic when you

- put off obligations by saying, "I forgot" or "I'm too busy right now" or "I'll do it later," even though you have little intention of ever following through

- ignore anything that challenges your thinking or lifestyle

- have little patience with ideas that don't fit in with yours

- believe the assignments and lectures in treatment don't apply to you—sometimes even before you've really looked at them

- twist statements that challenge your thinking around in your mind until you mistakenly believe they actually support your thinking

- pretend to listen by looking at the speaker and nodding or agreeing, while you are really thinking about other things that are more satisfying to you

- try to shift the responsibility for your lack of attention by claiming the speaker wasn't being clear

Facilitator Note

Encourage participants to come up with examples of selective memory and attention. This might best be achieved during group session since this tactic is easily recognizable in others.

TACTIC 7:

Minimizing (Trivializing)

Minimizing, or trivializing, begins in your mind as a way to block out thoughts of your wrongdoing and deny the full extent of the harm you have caused others. Instead of denying what you did, you try to make it seem trivial or less significant than it is. You minimize when you

- play down the importance of a situation
- view your offenses as less serious than others do
- minimize the harm of your actions when you are held accountable
- claim you didn't *intend* to cause so much harm

Here are some examples of minimizing:

- "I just got into a little trouble."
- "It was a mistake—I was just playing a prank."
- "I caught a case" or "I found myself in a situation."
- "I only dealt a little crack. It's not like I used it."
- "I only did it a few times." (When in fact you've done it seven, eight, or more times, which would be "several" or "a lot," not "a few.")

■

You have probably used all of these avoidance tactics at one time or another. In fact, you probably are using many of them in your treatment program right now.

Minimizing, or trivializing, begins in your mind as a way to block out thoughts of your wrongdoing.

EXERCISE **83** EXERCISE

Identifying Your Avoidance Strategies

➤ Choose two tactics from the list of avoidance strategies on page 268 that you used *before* you were incarcerated this most recent time. Give a detailed example of how you used each tactic. Include what you hoped would happen when you used those tactics (how you hoped others would react, what you hoped to avoid, or what advantage you thought you'd gain).

EXAMPLE:

Avoidance tactic	How you used this tactic and what you hoped to gain by it
#2 Being deliberately vague	When I was out doing a job—burglaries or whatever—and my wife would ask where I'd been, I'd just say I'd picked up some day work with some guys. If she pushed for details, I'd get mad and accuse her of not trusting me. I wanted her to back off so she wouldn't find out I was doing crime again and get pissed off at me.

1. Avoidance tactic

_____

How you used this tactic and what you hoped to gain by it

_____

_____

_____

_____

2. Avoidance tactic

_____

How you used this tactic and what you hoped to gain by it

_____

_____

_____

_____

➤ Now write down two avoidance strategies you have used in treatment and give an example of how you've used each one. Explain what you hoped to get out of using that strategy each time.

1. Avoidance tactic

_____

How you used this tactic and what you hoped to gain by it

_____

_____

_____

_____

2. Avoidance tactic

_____

How you used this tactic and what you hoped to gain by it

_____

_____

_____

_____

Diversion Strategies

The second category of criminal and addictive tactics is *diversion strategies*. Again, diversion strategies are the tactics you use to confuse others, to misdirect attention away from yourself or from the most important issues, and to avoid exposure by keeping those around you off balance and distracted. You use diversion strategies for the same reasons you use all other tactics:

to help you continue an irresponsible way of thinking and living.

The seven basic tactics you use to divert attention from the work you need to do to change and the things you need to be accountable for are listed on the next page. (We've numbered them 8–14 to pick up where we left off with the avoidance strategies.)

8. pointing out the faults of others

9. magnifying (exaggerating significance)

10. deliberately trying to confuse

11. quibbling over words

12. introducing irrelevant issues

13. discussing smokescreen issues

14. using self-shaming to avoid responsibility

TACTIC 8:

Pointing Out the Faults of Others

One way you divert attention from your wrongdoings and from your criminal and addictive thinking is to *point out the faults and failures of others*. As long as you can keep the focus on someone else—"I'm not as bad as *he* is; *he's* the one who has got a lot of work to do"—you think you can get away with not taking responsibility for what you need to change. You point out the faults of your peers, your family, staff, administrators, the commissioner of corrections, the president of the United States—it doesn't matter who—because the purpose is to keep the focus on anyone other than you.

You are pointing out the faults of others as a criminal tactic when you

- make a big issue over a mistake made by staff

- get overly involved in giving critical feedback in group to peers in order to use up all the time and not allow the group an opportunity to give you critical feedback

- talk behind people's backs (backbiting) in order to get others focused on everyone else's shortcomings and issues and not yours

- criticize the appearance of others

Facilitator Note
It is very helpful to post the list of seven diversion tactics in plain view of all participants at all times. You may choose to write these diversion tactics on a flip chart or on posters that can be used during each session. Creating these posters or flip charts could be an art project for the participants.

TACTIC 9:

Magnifying (Exaggerating Significance)

Magnifying, or *exaggerating the significance,* of minor issues is a tactic you use to justify your behavior or divert attention from your own issues. Stirring up debate or conflict over small matters can also give you a sense of control and some easy thrills. You use this tactic just to see how far you can push somebody (giving you a feeling of power), to distract others, and to put others on the defensive. You take little things and blow them out of proportion.

You are using the magnifying criminal tactic as a diversion when you

- point out the small inconsistencies of others and then dwell on them

- try to start conflicts between peers or between staff and peers over minor issues

- keep the attention on others in the group by arguing with them about what they've shared, rather than just giving appropriate feedback

- go on and on about something good you've done or all the progress you've made in order to keep the focus off the work you still have to do

- play up the shortcomings of others while ignoring their genuine efforts at change

- exaggerate the fault of the other person in a conflict in order to make your role in the conflict seem less significant than it really is

Facilitator Note

Encourage participants to come up with examples of magnifying, or exaggerating the significance. This might best be achieved during group session since this tactic is easily recognizable in others.

TACTIC 10:

Deliberately Trying to Confuse

As a criminal and addictive thinker, you will sometimes *try to confuse* others in order to get the upper hand. Keeping others confused is a way of maintaining your sense of power and diverting attention from yourself and the important issues at hand. This tactic once again reveals how little respect you have for the truth. In fact, you use this tactic in part because you mistakenly believe the truth is your enemy.

You are deliberately trying to confuse others when you

- offer inconsistent versions of an event

- make serious points but, when challenged, say you were only joking

- jump around quickly from point to point

- speak so fast that others can't follow your words

- speak so slowly that others can't maintain interest in what you're saying

- use street language, personal slang, double-talk, or fancy words so that others won't be sure what you're really saying (in such cases, you are usually saying nothing)

- alter written material by changing dates or other key information

- misquote others by twisting the meaning of their words or claiming they said things they never said

- when challenged on a discrepancy or inconsistency, claim the listener misunderstood, thereby shifting the burden to the other person

- stop in the middle of a story, admit you were lying, and claim you're now going to tell the whole truth, when in fact you have no such intention

Facilitator Note

Encourage participants to come up with examples of deliberately trying to confuse. This might best be achieved during group session since this tactic is easily recognizable in others.

TACTIC 11:

Quibbling over Words

Quibbling over words is a way not only to divert attention from more important things but also to make yourself appear smart in front of peers or staff. By disputing the meaning of words or phrases someone else uses rather than trying to understand that person, you take control of the conversation by knocking it off track.

You are quibbling over words when you

- say, "I don't understand what you mean when you use that word that way"

- say, "What you say is incorrect—that phrase means [this] and not [that]"

- argue over the exact language used rather than trying to clarify the exact meaning intended

- misquote someone and then make a big deal claiming your version is correct

- if a staff member asks you if you know anything about the assault out on the yard, you say, "I didn't see the assault," even though you may know exactly who did it and why (you just didn't see the actual assault)

TACTIC 12:

Introducing Irrelevant Issues

Another tactic you use to divert attention away from your-self and your criminal and addictive behavior is *introducing irrelevant issues*. You may try to direct discussion toward things that interest you, such as cars, sports, politics, or music—anything to avoid discussing your crimes and your criminal and addictive thinking patterns. You may introduce your personal history—family troubles or social disadvantages growing up—to distract others from your recent behavior. Or you may introduce race, one of the most sensitive issues in this society and especially behind bars (as you know). As a criminal and an addict, you use race in order to justify, excuse, or keep the focus away from your behavior. And yes, race can be and is used as a diversion strategy by people of *all* races—including yours.

The fact is, your interests, your personal history, and race *are* important issues, and they deserve thought and discussion, but only in an appropriate way and time. Using them in any way to avoid looking at and changing your criminal and addictive thinking and behavior is introducing irrelevant issues. Like all the other tactics, its purpose is to allow you to keep thinking and living the way you have been—to avoid change.

You are introducing irrelevant issues when you

- use race to present yourself as a victim, thereby refusing to admit how you have been the victimizer

- charge racism when you don't get your own way or when your other tactics don't work and others continue to confront you

- constantly talk about your rights in order to avoid talking about your "wrongs"

Facilitator Note

Encourage participants to come up with examples of introducing irrelevant issues. This might best be achieved during group session since this tactic is easily recognizable in others.

- justify your crimes and alcohol and drug use with sad stories of how hard you've had it in life; even if the stories are true, they don't excuse your personal behavior and choices

- try to start arguments about other subjects when you are confronted by family, therapists, or peers

- blame your behavior choices on social injustice

TACTIC 13:

Discussing Smokescreen Issues

Smokescreen issues are slightly different from irrelevant issues. Smokescreen issues may be treatment issues that you use at inappropriate times in order to avoid disclosure. For example, you focus on some family issues in chemical dependency group or on your addiction in the family group.

Another form of using smokescreen issues is picking just one issue and keeping the discussion about your behavior as it relates to that issue at all times. If you have been diagnosed as depressed, you may talk about nothing else except your depression. It becomes a smokescreen issue when you use it to keep attention away from your criminal and addictive thinking and behavior. You say that if only you could take care of the depression, then you could really take advantage of the program and change. It's not that your depression is irrelevant to your thinking and behavior, it's that it is only one part of it.

You are using smokescreen issues when you

- keep writing the same Thinking Reports over and over

- discuss treatment issues in the wrong group or at the wrong time to keep from focusing on the subject at hand

- introduce physical or mental health problems just to excuse you from treatment work

Facilitator Note
Encourage participants to come up with examples of smokescreen issues. This might best be achieved during group session since this tactic is easily recognizable in others.

TACTIC 14:

Using Self-Shaming to Avoid Responsibility

For those who prefer the diversion tactics, *using self-shaming to avoid responsibility* is often a last resort. When you are backed into a corner, you try to avoid taking a hard look at your behavior and thinking by shaming yourself publicly. You think that if you beat yourself up enough in front of peers and therapists, they'll let you off the hook. Or you may continually claim that your unresolved shame issues must be addressed before you can do the work at hand.

This diversion tactic should not be confused with your legitimate issues. The important difference between the two is the *reason* you are bringing up your feelings of shame. Are you just trying to distract attention or are you sincerely asking for help? Asking for help with shame issues is appropriate—at the right time and with the right person. Treatment, however, is not about shame. It's about *change.*

Self-shaming can be just another way to keep the attention of others off the fact that you still haven't done the work. Your self-shaming may be genuine or it may just be an act. It doesn't matter: Either way, you still haven't looked hard at your thinking and behavior and disclosed it to the group. You still haven't tried to make changes in how you think and live. You still haven't gotten honest.

You use self-shaming when you

- admit to and dwell on one crime or behavior to hide more serious ones

- talk and talk about what an awful person you are to get pity from others

Facilitator Note
Encourage participants to come up with examples of using self-shaming to avoid responsibility. This might best be achieved during group session since this tactic is easily recognizable in others.

Identifying Your Diversion Strategies

➤ Choose three tactics that you have used from the list of diversion strategies. Give a detailed example of how you used each tactic. Include what you hoped would happen when you used those tactics (how you hoped others would react, what you hoped to divert attention from, or what advantage you thought you'd gain).

EXAMPLE:

Diversion tactic	How you used this tactic and what you hoped to gain by it
#9 Magnifying (exaggerating significance)	When my cellmate took a pen from me without asking and I caught him using it working on one of the workbook exercises, I made a big deal about him disrespecting me and my property. But the thing is, I didn't really give a damn about the pen. I was just trying to rile things up and put it on him so I'd look good.

1. Diversion tactic

_____

How you used this tactic and what you hoped to gain by it

_____

_____

_____

_____

2. Diversion tactic

_____

How you used this tactic and what you hoped to gain by it

_____

_____

_____

_____

3. Diversion tactic

_____

How you used this tactic and what you hoped to gain by it

_____

_____

_____

_____

Aggression Strategies

To review, you use *aggression strategies* to attack, intimidate, and undermine the legitimate efforts of others. You actively try to create chaos through stirring up conflict, resentment, and other hard feelings. You take on the victim role, saying that others provoked you or at least didn't get out of your way. You tell yourself, then, that they are just getting what they deserve. You also try to make others fear you so they won't challenge your addictive and criminal thinking. Again, your main goals with aggression strategies are getting what you want, avoiding exposure and the zero state by keeping others on the defensive, and responding when you think you have been provoked or made to look bad.

The seven basic aggression strategies that criminals use to prevent others from confronting their thinking and behavior are listed below.

(We've numbered them 15–21 to pick up where we left off with the diversion strategies.)

15. arguing
16. using threatening words or behaviors (veiled or direct)
17. raging
18. sarcasm and teasing
19. splitting staff
20. creating chaos
21. attention seeking

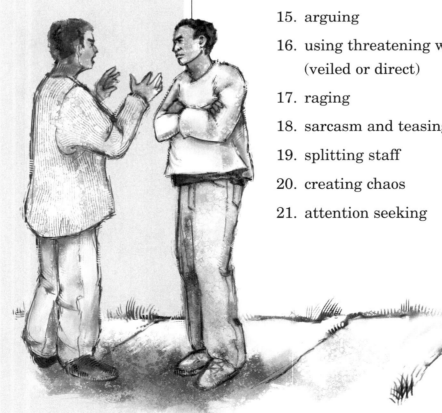

TACTIC 15:

Arguing

Arguing is an aggressive criminal and addictive tactic you use to keep your distance from others and to get what you want. It is yet another strategy you have for protecting your criminal and addictive way of life.

Arguing turns a ***dialogue*** of ideas into just a war of words. Nobody learns anything new in an argument because arguing is not about learning, it's about winning. That means its only purpose is to pump up your ego and humiliate the other person.

> **Dialogue**
>
> *Dialogue* is an exchange of ideas and opinions between two equals. The most important aspect of dialogue is that it is an *exchange.* That means ideas and opinions flow both ways and are taken in and considered by both people.

You are using arguing as an aggressive criminal and addictive tactic when you

- raise your voice in a discussion, feel the adrenaline rush of battle, and focus only on proving the other person wrong

- refuse to listen to or think about what others are saying

- turn meanings around and attack (with words) the points of view of others

- try to turn the tables when you are confronted for not living up to an agreement by arguing that the other person misunderstood the agreement

- use anger and intensity to try to overpower others in a discussion and avoid having to look honestly at your deeper thoughts and fears

- turn conversations (dialogues) into power struggles and insist on having the last word

TACTIC 16:

Using Threatening Words or Behaviors (Veiled or Direct)

You use two types of *threatening words* and *behaviors* to try to control others, *veiled* and *direct*. Veiled threats are more hidden. They may include intimidating body language, such as threatening stares ("mean mugging") or flexing muscles in your arms and neck or clenching your fists. Veiled threats could also be vague statements that suggest "something bad" might happen to someone.

Direct threatening words and behaviors are more out in the open and include physical intimidation or statements of intent to cause harm. You use them to reinforce your feelings of superiority and entitlement and to avoid putdowns.

You are using veiled threatening words and behaviors when you

- say, "If I wasn't in this program trying to get healthy, you wouldn't be talking like that for long"
- say, "Where are the grievance forms?"
- say, "Remember what you did last weekend? It would be unfortunate if the staff found out"
- say, "My brothers ain't going to like that"
- use "mean mugging" or other threatening body language

You are using direct threatening words and behaviors when you

- hit or push someone
- say, "You're a dead man—my brothers will see to that"
- say, "Let's step into the bathroom where we can settle this like men"
- stand over someone flexing your muscles, staring, and making fists

- physically back someone down

- stalk others

- prey on the vulnerabilities of others

- curse at others

TACTIC 17:

Raging

You use *raging* as a tactic when you let yourself go wild with anger—yelling and screaming and threatening and throwing things (behavior guaranteed to put you in seg or get you thrown out of the program). You also use raging when you suggest that if someone doesn't leave you alone, you could explode at any time. You tell "war stories" about all the people you have beat up because you have a short fuse and can't control yourself. Raging is another way you attempt to control others—by making them keep their distance and making them afraid of you. You believe that someone who is afraid of you won't confront your criminal and addictive ways.

You are raging when you

- lose all control in anger and become wild and destructive

- make others believe you *could* lose all control and fly into a rage at any time, so they'd better treat you very carefully

Raging is another way you attempt to control others—by making them keep their distance and making them afraid of you.

Facilitator Note
Raging, which may appear spontaneous, is a premeditated tactic. Offenders will carefully consider when, where, and with whom to go into a rage to get what they want. Offenders who may rage in front of more vulnerable peers or staff will never rage in front of someone more threatening and dangerous than they are. The point of raging is to physically or emotionally intimidate another in order to get something.

Facilitator Note
Encourage participants to come up with examples of raging. This might best be achieved during group session since this tactic is easily recognizable in others.

TACTIC 18:

Sarcasm and Teasing

Sarcasm is sharp and mean-spirited language used to make others look stupid or worthless. You use it as an aggression tactic to build yourself up by putting others down. Sarcasm and *teasing* are strategies designed to control others by keeping them on the defensive. As with all aggression strategies, they are efforts to make you feel powerful and warn others to keep their distance.

You are using sarcasm and teasing when you

- are sharply critical and unforgiving when others slip up

- try to create an image of cool for yourself by making others appear foolish

- pick on others for their appearance or the way they talk

- try to embarrass, demean, or make fun of another with little digs or insults

- say, "I guess you wouldn't happen to know that . . ." in order to make someone look dumb

TACTIC 19:

Splitting Staff

Splitting staff is a common aggressive tactic used by people who are incarcerated and in treatment programs. Splitting staff is a variation of the old military strategy "divide and conquer." By trying to pit one staff member against another, you hope to decrease their authority and effectiveness and increase your influence and power. Lost in this game, of course, is any hope of your doing the treatment work and making the changes that could keep you out of prison and help you live responsibly in the world.

You are splitting staff when you

- tell one staff member, "You really understand me, unlike those other therapists"

- complain that staff members never explain things clearly, except for one or two particular therapists

- attack a staff member by saying, "You're the worst therapist here. All the others are better than you"

- twist stories around so one staff member will think that another is being unfair to you

- tell different versions of an incident to different staff members to try to put them in conflict

- go "staff shopping" until one finally gives you the answer you want

You may also use the splitting staff tactic to split your peer group. You are splitting peer groups when you

- say, "I can do treatment with him, but not with *that* guy"

- try to drum up support for yourself by "gathering a posse" while putting others down behind their backs

- try to purposely ruin someone's reputation by spreading rumors

Facilitator Note

Encourage participants to come up with examples of splitting staff. This might best be achieved during group session since this tactic is easily recognizable in others.

TACTIC 20:

Creating Chaos

You are *creating chaos* as a tactic when you use a combination of other tactics to cause a constant disruption of programs, groups, exercises, and life on the unit. You may be spreading rumors (even about yourself) while you try to split staff, attack peers behind their backs, threaten peers in and out of group, accuse others of misunderstanding you, change your story depending on who is listening, argue over everything, and demand your rights. The idea is to keep the staff so busy dealing with the messes you make that the program grinds to a halt.

You create chaos in order to

- avoid working on your thinking and behavior and making changes

- get pleasure from the feeling of power and control it gives you

- feel like a big shot, that no treatment program is ever going to change *you*

TACTIC 21:

Attention Seeking

Attention seeking becomes an aggressive tactic anytime it disrupts the efforts of others to work the treatment program. Often you use bizarre or shocking behaviors or disclosures to stir things up.

You are using attention seeking as an aggressive criminal and addictive tactic when you

- threaten to quit the program

- do outrageous things to stand out and grab the group's attention or to intentionally upset people

- dress to show off a gang tattoo or muscles

- walk around like you are big, bad, and nationwide

- aggressively refuse to comply with staff

Identifying Your Aggression Strategies

➤ Choose two tactics that you have used from the list of aggression strategies. Give a detailed example of how you used each tactic. Include what you hoped would happen when you used those tactics (how you hoped others would react, what you hoped to divert attention from, or what advantage you thought you'd gain).

Facilitator Note
Review the aggression strategies on page 288. This will make it easier for participants to complete exercise 85.

EXAMPLE:

Aggression tactic	How you used this tactic and what you hoped to gain by it
#18 Sarcasm and teasing	When X asked what "strategy" meant, I laughed out loud and said to the guy next to me, "They must not of gotten to that in the second grade," and I said it loud enough so several people around me could hear. I wanted to make X look like an idiot and make me look smart. I did it because it felt good to put him down. It also showed everybody I'm a hardass, so let me be.

1. Aggression tactic

_____

How you used this tactic and what you hoped to gain by it

_____

_____

_____

_____

2. Aggression tactic

_____

How you used this tactic and what you hoped to gain by it

_____

_____

_____

_____

Switching Strategies

As a criminal and addictive thinker, you have particular tactics you prefer. You may especially like aggression strategies because they seem to give you what you want most. Or you may be the type that thinks lying low—using avoidance strategies—is the most effective way of keeping people off your back and allowing you to continue your criminal and addictive lifestyle.

When your favorite tactics don't work, however, you will readily switch to another type to get what you want: power, control, and avoiding responsibility, accountability, and change. For example, some criminals and addicts who use avoidance strategies and appear passive will switch over immediately to aggressive, threatening tactics in a situation as soon as they figure out that the avoidance tactics aren't working. Understanding how you use all these tactics will help you begin to stop them and to find new behaviors that are more effective in getting along in the world.

Sometimes you may work your way "up the ladder," starting with avoidance, moving to diversion, and then getting aggressive. Sometimes you may use many strategies from all three groups in the space of just minutes! This is most likely to occur when you believe you aren't getting what you deserve, you are stressed out and feel cornered, or when you fear going into the zero state.

EXERCISE **86** EXERCISE

Identifying Your Pattern of Criminal and Addictive Tactics

➤ Which category of tactics—avoidance, diversion, or aggression strategies—do you use first?

_____

➤ Which tactics in that category are your favorites?

1. _____

_____

2. _____

_____

3. _____

_____

Facilitator Note
Participants will need to refer back to page 266, "How You Use Tactics," in order to complete exercise 86.

➤ When that type of tactic doesn't work for you, which of the other two categories do you switch to first?

_____

➤ What are your favorite tactics in this second category?

1. _____

   _____

2. _____

   _____

3. _____

   _____

➤ Are the tactics you used on the outside the same as what you tend to use on the inside? Why or why not?

_____

_____

_____

By understanding your use of criminal and addictive tactics and the thinking behind each of them, you can better understand and begin to change your criminal, irresponsible, and antisocial behavior. Now you are ready to start filling out the Tactics part on your Thinking Report on page 179.

Conclusion

Congratulations. By completing this workbook, you've learned that it is possible to change your thinking. This is good news. You now recognize that you have your own personal mental map that will give you direction and guide your behavior. Your personal mental map helps guide you through life.

This workbook has helped you learn how to think about your thinking. You've learned how to replace old patterns of thinking. A happier, healthier, more free way of life awaits you. And only you can make that happen.

Facilitator Note
Refer back to the Thinking Report on page 179 of this workbook. The participants should now be ready to add tactics to their Thinking Report.

Andrews, D. A., and James Bonta. *The Psychology of Criminal Conduct.* 2d ed. Cincinnati, Ohio: Anderson Publishing Co., 1998.

Beck, Aaron. *Prisoners of Hate: The Cognitive Basis of Anger, Hostility, and Violence.* New York: HarperCollins, 1999.

Beck, Aaron, Arthur Freeman, and Associates. *Cognitive Therapy of Personality Disorders.* New York: The Guilford Press, 1990.

Beck, Judith. *Cognitive Therapy: Basics and Beyond.* New York: The Guilford Press, 1995.

Burns, David D. *Feeling Good: The New Mood Therapy.* Revised. New York: Avon Books, Inc., 1999.

———. *The Feeling Good Handbook.* Revised. New York: Penguin Putman, Inc., 1999.

Greenberger, Dennis. *Mind Over Mood: Change How You Feel by Changing the Way You Think.* New York: The Guilford Press, 1995.

Jones, Dan. *Words for Our Feelings.* Austin, Tex.: Mandala, 1992.

Millon, Theodore, and Erik Siminsen, Morten Birket-Smith, Roger D. Davis, eds. *Psychopathy: Antisocial, Criminal, and Violent Behavior.* The Guilford Press: New York, 1998.

Nakken, Craig. *The Addictive Personality: Understanding the Addictive Process and Compulsive Behavior.* Center City, Minn.: Hazelden Publishing, 1996.

Samenow, Stanton E. *Inside the Criminal Mind.* New York: Times Books, 1984.

Twerski, Abraham J. *Addictive Thinking: Understanding Self-Deception.* 2d ed. Center City, Minn.: Hazelden Publishing, 1997.

Yochelson, Samuel, and Stanton E. Sameow. *The Criminal Personality: A Profile for Change.* Vol. 1. Northvale, N.J.: Jason Aronson, 1976.

———. *The Criminal Personality: The Change Process.* Vol. 2. Northvale, N.J.: Jason Aronson, 1977.

———. *The Criminal Personality: The Drug User.* Vol. 3. Northvale, N.J.: Jason Aronson, 1986.

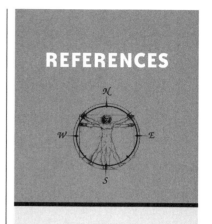

REFERENCES

A NEW DIRECTION

A Cognitive-Behavioral Treatment Curriculum

Thinking Report

1. Event _____

   _____

2. Thoughts _____

   _____

3. Feelings _____

   _____

4. Behavior _____

   _____

5. Can you identify a core belief? _____

   _____

6. Alternative thoughts _____

   _____

7. Alternative behavior _____

   _____

Thinking distortions _____

Thinking patterns _____

Tactics _____